Johnny Podres

Brooklyn's Only Yankee Killer

by

Bob, John and Robert S. Bennett

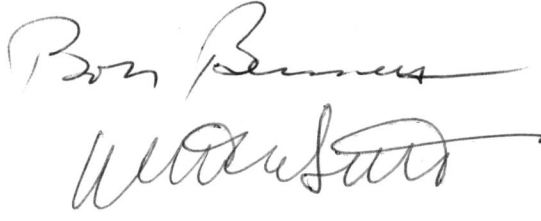

1663 LIBERTY DRIVE, SUITE 200
BLOOMINGTON, INDIANA 47403
(800) 839-8640
WWW.AUTHORHOUSE.COM

© 2005 Bob, John and Robert S. Bennett. All Rights Reserved.

No part of this book may be reproduced, stored in a retrieval system, or transmitted by any means without the written permission of the author.

First published by AuthorHouse 02/28/05

ISBN: 1-4208-3541-6 (sc)
ISBN: 1-4208-3542-4 (dj)

Library of Congress Control Number: 2005901848

Printed in the United States of America
Bloomington, Indiana

This book is printed on acid-free paper.

Cover Photo © Bettmann/CORBIS

This book is dedicated to everyone in Brooklyn who celebrated the 1955 World Champions.

Contents

Acknowledgements ix
Foreword xi
Chapter One Now Pitching for the Dodgers:
A Decade of Misery and Pain 1
Chapter Two Killing the Yankees. Again. 7
Chapter Three Just Like His Father 15
Chapter Four Three Years on the Big Club 21
Chapter Five "Thanks, Whitey!" 39
Chapter Six Beatified in Brooklyn 51
Chapter Seven From Swabby to Shut-out and ERA King 61
Chapter Eight Way Out West 67
Chapter Nine Victories and Tragedy 83
Chapter Ten The Dodgers 'Big Three' 91
Chapter Eleven Bring on the Yankees 111
Chapter Twelve Life After L.A. 125
Chapter Thirteen Buzzie Comes Through 131
Chapter Fourteen Time for Reflection 139
Afterword 143
Appendix Johnny Podres' Statistics 145

Acknowledgements

The authors would like to thank the following people who contributed recollections and observations that enriched our account of the life of Johnny Podres. They include E.J. (Buzzie) Bavasi, Yogi Berra, Larry Burright, Chuck Churn, Roger Craig, Don Demeter, Larry Dierker, Al Downing, Chuck Essegian, Al Ferrara, Jim Fregosi, Preston Gomez, Dick Gray, Joan Hodges, Clem Labine, Jim Landis, Norm Larker, Ken Lehman, Hector Lopez, Mike Marshall, Danny McDevitt, Gil McDougald, Ken McMullen, Glenn Mickens, Wally Moon, Bobby Morgan, Irv Noren, Claude Osteen, Ed Palmquist, Joe Pignatano, John Purdin, Bobby Richardson, Pete Richert, Ken Rowe, Bob Shaw, Larry Sherry, Norm Sherry, Gerry Staley, Don Thompson, Jeff Torborg, Dave Wickersham, Mitch (Wild Thing) Williams, Stan Williams and Gordon Windhorn.

Special thanks go to Joan Podres, who provided a great deal of information and documentation, including a scrapbook compiled by Alyce Mace in 1955. Red Sox fan Alice Bennett deserves gratitude for her suggestions and patience throughout the writing and production of this book. For more information on the 50th anniversary of the 1955 World Series, go to www.johnnypodres.com.

Foreword

The first time I saw Johnny Podres, I remember very well, he was pitching for Hazard, Kentucky, in 1951. I liked what I saw and as the general manager I brought him up to the Dodgers in 1953.

I've said it hundreds of times and I will say it again:

Even though I had the greatest pitcher in the game, Sandy Koufax; then Don Drysdale, Don Newcombe and others, *if I had to win one game and my life depended on that game*, Johnny Podres was my man.

Many times during regular season games he proved he was a big game "money pitcher." As an example, I remember one day in St. Louis when we just had to win to stay ahead in the race. I was sitting in a box seat with team physician Dr. Robert Kerlan before the game and John came by.

"Why are you guys looking so worried?" he asked. "I'll shut the bastards out."

He didn't shut them out but he did beat them, 2-1. That was his attitude every time he got the ball. And he certainly proved he could do it in the World Series, when he did shut them out.

Off the field, he was one of my favorites, in spite or perhaps because of some of his escapades and antics. Johnny and his pal Don Zimmer were in Detroit on an off day and were going to the racetrack. John called me in Los Angeles and said, "Buzzie, we got a tip on a horse that should pay at least 7-1. How much should I put on it for you?"

Nothing, I said.

With that, Zimmer gets on the phone. "Buzzie, this is a good thing. John and I each owe you $100. Why don't we bet the $200 for you?"

Reluctantly, I said okay. Then I hung up the phone and told my secretary I had just lost $200.

"How do you know? It's only 12 o'clock in Detroit and the races haven't started yet."

At three o'clock in Detroit John called and said, "Buzzie, you won't believe this. The horse went off at 12-1 and just got nipped at the wire."

That happened some 40 years ago and it wasn't the first or the last time. I still don't know the name of that horse.

Regardless, Pod and Zim are the best, but if I had the money those two jokers owe me I would have retired five years early.

Johnny was with me for 15 years in the minors and the majors until 1966 when the Dodgers had a great starting four of Koufax, Drysdale, Claude Osteen and Don Sutton. I traded John, to Detroit, because Jim Campbell was the general manager and a close friend who promised to take good care of him. In 1969, I was with the Padres. As I usually did with players I really cared about, I brought John back with me.

When you read this book about the inspirational and amazing life and times of Johnny Podres, a great friend for more than half a century, you will be reading about a fine major league pitcher who gave 100 percent all of the time. And one who still owes me money.

-- E.J. (Buzzie) Bavasi

Emil J. "Buzzie" Bavasi is one of baseball's legendary and longest-serving executives. He was born in 1914 and began his career with the Brooklyn Dodgers under Larry MacPhail in 1939. Following a stint in the military as an infantry machine gunner from 1943-46, Bavasi served as general manager of the Dodgers' Triple-A farm club in Montreal. In 1951, as soon as Walter O'Malley took over ownership of the team from Branch Rickey, Bavasi was appointed vice president and general manager. He held this position through the club's move to Los Angeles until he resigned in June 1968 to become general manager and part owner of the expansion San Diego Padres. From 1978 - 1984, he served as general manager of the California and Anaheim Angels. In 1978, he became a member of Baseball's Hall of Fame Veterans Committee. He is currently the senior partner emeritus with Bavasi Sports Partners, a family business that includes his sons Peter (a former Padres' general manager, founding president of the Toronto Blue Jays, and former president of the Cleveland Indians), Bob (owner and operator of the Everett AquaSox from 1984-98), Chris (a six-term mayor of Flagstaff, Arizona) and Bill (a former general manager of the Anaheim Angels and currently general manager of the Seattle Mariners), and daughter-in-law Margaret. His autobiography, Off the Record, *was published in 1987.*

Chapter One
Now Pitching for the Dodgers:
A Decade of Misery and Pain

When a baseball team loses 10-0, languishes in the second division all season and secures the cellar year after year, its fans sigh and laugh it all off. It's so sorry it's funny.

But what if your team, over a 10-year span, comes within a hanging curveball of winning almost every time but winds up with nothing to show for it except a gargantuan reputation as chokers? What else would you call a team that lost a pennant or a playoff or a World Series in its last game of the season for five straight years—and seven of the previous eight?

To fully appreciate the role Johnny Podres played in rewriting forever the sorry script of the Brooklyn Dodgers, we have to recall the drama that played out before he arrived on the scene.

Brooklyn residents of the first half of the 20th century arguably identified with their team more closely than those of any other. The borough was largely a diverse but close community of first- and second-generation immigrants unified by their team, in large part to prove that love of America's pastime would help to make them truly American themselves. They came to the Brooklyn melting pot from all over Europe and elsewhere, and brought with them a variety of religious customs, but were unanimous in their devotion to the Dodgers, whom they worshiped at an edifice called Ebbets Field, built in a former farming section once known as Pigtown. The players lived among them, in their neighborhoods.

Some Brooklynites even took Dodgers into their own homes in those days when low player salaries wouldn't supply a hotel room.

What did the fans get in return for their unqualified adoration at the Ebbets altar? The ungrateful team branded them second-class citizens of the nation's largest city, or even, like the players, just bums.

In fact, admission of Brooklyn origin was fodder for stand-up comics' best jokes. If the borough had still been the independent city it was before absorption into New York City years earlier, it would have been the third largest in the United States, but movie and television script writers regularly made Brooklyn a source of derisive laughter. Some television sitcoms, such as those with Jackie Gleason and Molly Goldberg, were even set in the borough to guarantee a lot of laughs. It was as if everyone in Brooklyn was named Rodney Dangerfield. They got no respect.

The Dodgers did field some magnificent position players, the original and celebrated "Boys of Summer," but they had a big problem. The pitchers were just not quite good enough.

Of course, those teams exceeded the accomplishments of those that preceded them. Since their beginnings in the 19th century, they had been mostly a joke. They were well known for having three of their base runners on the same bag. They bore lots of unflattering names, including the "Daffiness Boys" and, mostly, the "Bums," a moniker with a mascot clownish hobo inspired in 1937 by a Brooklyn cab driver and created by cartoonist Willard Mullin. Even when they won the pennant in 1941, for the first time in 21 years, catcher Mickey Owen dropped a third strike that led to eventual loss of the World Series to the Yankees. The following year they won 104 games, but rookie Stan Musial led the Cardinals to 106 and the pennant. During the ensuing war years they finished third in '43 and seventh in '44, but rebounded to third in '45, when the Cubs took the National League flag.

Then things started to get serious. And frustrating. In truth, they became agonizing and miserable.

Recently, followers of the Cubs, and also the Red Sox, have complained because their teams failed to win a World Series in many years—not even in the lifetimes of most of their fans. Sox fans quit griping only in 2004. The Dodgers had *never* won, and the Dodgers were one of the oldest teams in the majors, dating back to the 1800s. What seemed even worse to their fans, including the teen-aged Johnny Podres, they came excruciatingly close time and again.

Take 1946, when they tied for the pennant but lost the first-ever National League playoff to the Cards. Consider '47, when with rookie Jackie Robinson they won the pennant but lost the World Series to the

Johnny Podres

Yankees again, in seven games. Or '48, when they finished third behind the Boston Braves and those Cards again (by one game).

In '49, the pitching of Don Newcombe, Ralph Branca, Carl Erskine and Preacher Roe came up short again. The pennant-winning Dodgers dropped the World Series to the Yankees, once more, in five games. Then in '50, tied for first with Philadelphia on the last day of the season, they watched Dick Sisler clout a 10th inning homer to give the Whiz Kids Phillies their first pennant since 1915.

Dodgers addicts imagined that was rock bottom, the depths of despair, with nowhere to go but up. They had another thought coming in 1951, thanks to their worst enemy. Those fans old enough to remember will never forget that their team owned a supposedly ironclad 13 ½-game lead on August 13 and blew it to a tie. No team had ever lost a lead of that size in baseball history. What was even worse, they lost it to the other half of the fiercest rivalry in the annals of major league ball. Then their beloved Bums rekindled hope for a day when they rebounded to put a three-game pennant playoff virtually in the bat bag.

After the Giants won the first game, at the Polo Grounds, 4-2, the Dodgers came back and shellacked them, 11-0, at Ebbets Field. After seven innings of game three, they were tied 1-1, but the Dodgers scored three times in the top of eighth, to take what looked like a commanding lead. Dodgers ace Newcombe was on the mound, and the pennant seemed sure.

Newcombe tired, however, and gave up successive singles, putting men on first and second. Another base hit scored a run so manager Charlie Dressen brought in Branca, who served up Bobby Thomson's cheap "shot heard 'round the world." It was a fly ball, a can of corn that would have fallen short of Fenway Park's "Green Monster." It barely cleared the left field wall of the Polo Grounds, a mere 279 feet from the plate, landing in the third row of seats.

The horrible hit occurred a few minutes after 4 p.m. on Wednesday, October 3. A half-hour earlier, when school got out, two teenaged boys raced to a downtown furniture store where the game was on television in the showroom window. One, a Dodgers fan, became so distraught by Thomson's homer that he paid off a quarter bet on the playoff with his best pal by throwing two dimes and a nickel into city traffic. Then he bade his buddy to "Go and get it, you son of a bitch." (Years later, the adult son of the sore loser told Thomson, "You ruined my father's life"—a bit of an overstatement—and a gracious Thomson apologized for that, but not for hitting the homer.) The father still has not completely put the event behind him over a half-century later. And he still hates the Giants.

Podres piled up league-high numbers of strikeouts and victories in the low minors in '51 but the next year he was still in Triple A and it was Dodgers déjà vu all over again. Rookie pitcher Joe Black led Brooklyn to a pennant-winning season over the Giants, for some measure of revenge. But neither Black nor Erskine or Preacher Roe could put those Yankees away in the seventh game of the World Series. As Dodgers announcer Vin Scully would put it, time and again, it was still close but no cigar.

The year that followed brought unprecedented pain. Fans who saw Rocky Mountain highs before Grand Canyon letdowns in the recent past now would find an even deeper chasm. The Dodgers won 105 games and lost only 49, for a winning percentage of .682. It was the first year a National League team defended its crown successfully since the '44 Cards. Brooklyn bested the runner-up Braves by 13 games.

League MVP catcher Roy Campanella paved the way. The Dodgers led the league in runs, homers and batting average. Their victory total reached an all-time team high. Duke Snider smacked 42 homers and Campy cracked 41. It was the first time a National League team fielded two players with more than 40. Right fielder Carl Furillo, called the "Reading Rifle" because of his powerful and accurate throwing arm, won the batting title. In fact, the Dodgers entered the Fall Classic with five players hitting over .300.

Pitching? Erskine won 20, Russ Meyer, Billy Loes, Roe and Clem Labine were all in double figures in wins. Rookie Johnny Podres, just 20 years old after a year at Montreal, compiled a 9-4 record with 82 strikeouts in 115 innings.

And there they were again—the Yankees. By now it was well accepted that a genuine World Series featured *only* the Dodgers *and* the Yankees. A Fall Classic that lacked both of these teams was merely a bargain-basement knock-off. After all, this Series would be the fifth between them since 1941, and New York then, as it remains today, was the media capital of the world. The hyperbole oozing from seven daily newspapers and four television networks made it appear that the two teams *owned* the World Series. Most of the rest of country was tired of this scenario, and, primarily, they resented the Yankees because they kept on winning it.

In '53, however, the Yankees would need a special effort, some thought, because of the huge numbers the Dodgers put up during the season. In Brooklyn the feeling was one of optimism tempered by experienced resignation. They hoped it would happen but they knew deep down that the Dodgers couldn't do it. The pitchers would fail in the end.

The reality was that Erskine couldn't end the futility, despite starting the first, third and (final) sixth game. Neither could Roe, Loes or Labine.

Nor could the rookie Podres, finally admitted to the mound by the fifth game and relieved after two and two-thirds innings of work but not before getting a hit and scoring a run. He allowed one hit, walked two and took the loss in a game that ended 11-7, with his team out-hitting the winners 14-11.

If there had ever been the slightest doubt that the invincible Bronx Bombers would forever defeat the hapless Brooklyn Bums, in 1953 it disappeared. Ultimate Yankees triumph was cast in bronze and carved in stone. It was Gospel. Only wild-eyed Dodger dreamers imagined anything different. The Yankees took the series in six, for their fifth straight world title. What had been widely regarded as the golden age of baseball, certainly in New York City, seemed instead to Dodgers fans an era fabricated of failure.

Today, half of the starting position players on that Dodgers squad are in the Hall of Fame. Plaques hang for Roy Campanella, Pee Wee Reese, Jackie Robinson and Duke Snider. There is still a chance for Gil Hodges, which would leave only third base and the outfield corners not represented in Cooperstown.

Pitchers? Not a single one.

During the '54 season, the highly touted Erskine was tagged with 15 losses against 18 wins. Newcombe won only nine, Roe only three. Branca was gone and Loes and Labine held promise but by now everybody knew that Brooklyn's frontline pitchers, despite regularly bringing their team to the top of their own league, couldn't beat the Yankees in the World Series. That year they didn't even get them there. The hated Giants finished first, five games ahead of runner-up Brooklyn.

The Dodgers did, however, have a promising 21-year-old left-hander, and as a fifth starter in '54, he compiled an 11-3 record with a pair of shutouts before undergoing an appendectomy in late June and taking four more losses. That was the year miler Roger Bannister broke the four-minute barrier and became the first *Sports Illustrated* magazine "Sportsman of the Year."

Nobody dreamed then that "wait 'til next year" would also mean finding a Dodger *pitcher* on that magazine cover with a second such accolade. That year it went to the Most Valuable Player of the 1955 World Series. Nobody imagined that this brash young lefty could lift an unbearable baseball burden from the shoulders of two million Brooklynites plus legions of Dodgers fans elsewhere.

Nobody knew the upstate upstart would transform a franchise of chokers into World Champions, restore self-esteem to an entire borough and blaze a triumphant trail for Brooklyn and Los Angeles Dodgers pitchers to follow. That's because nobody knew that Johnny Podres would replace agony with ecstasy and kill the Yankees.

It would be different for future hurlers, from Sandy Koufax and Don Drysdale to Don Sutton (all in Cooperstown) and more to come, because Podres assumed a pivotal position on the Dodgers mound. He would map new Dodgers territory all the way to Los Angeles. For the first time in the history of the franchise, it would be possible for Dodgers pitchers actually to envision ultimate World Series victory. Because he broke the ice and melted a major league inferiority complex, "next year" finally would arrive and return again and again. Because of Podres, who would go on to collect *four* World Series Championship rings as a Dodgers pitcher, the *New York Daily News* front-page headline did not ask, but exclaimed in type size ordinarily reserved for Pearl Harbor invasions or nuclear bomb drops,

"WHO'S A BUM!"

Brooklyn-born and bred, Al Ferrara was 15 years old in 1955, and like thousands of other youngsters his age, suffered since first grade along with the Dodgers. Fifty years later, here's what he remembered:

"All of us Brooklynites had this problem with the Yankees. We had a great team that just fell short every year to another great team. It was depressing and you knew we would be saying 'Wait 'til next year.'

"It came!

"I remember missing school that day to watch the game. Johnny Podres was not the ace of that staff. We would have to score a lot of runs. He had beaten them earlier in the series. No way again. Mid-game I was hopeful but—it always happens. Looper down the left field line. Amoros catches it. No way!! Gil stretching for the final out.

"We are delivered by a heart and a great change-up—a hero for all of Brooklyn—Johnny Podres. The Deliverer. Big Party!!!

"Little did I know then that I would be his roommate eight years later in Los Angeles (as Al, the 'bull," a Dodgers outfielder). I have often told him, 'If you beat the Indians no one would know who you are. But you beat the Yankees'!"

Chapter Two
Killing the Yankees. Again.

Las Vegas odds makers anointed the New York Yankees as 8-5 favorites to beat the Los Angeles Dodgers in the 1963 World Series. Taking a different view, Johnny Podres told the press: "We'll win it in five. No, better change that. We might do it in four."

As 66,455 fans watched, 31-year-old Podres loosened up on the sidelines. His appearance at Yankee Stadium was his first since 1955, causing Yankee fans to cringe as they recalled his earlier performance. Alongside him was Yankees pitcher Al Downing, a 22-year-old rookie southpaw. During pre-game press photographs, Downing looked nervous. But Podres, ready for his fourth Fall Classic, told him: "This is the World Series—enjoy it." It was Thursday, October 3, 1963, one o'clock in the afternoon, the second game, bright and sunny, with a temperature of 80 degrees.

Downing's mates hardly enjoyed Game One. Sandy Koufax defeated Whitey Ford and the Yankees, 5-2, striking out Mickey Mantle, Bobby Richardson, Tony Kubek and Tom Tresh twice, and Roger Maris once. In the bottom of the ninth inning with two outs, Yankees fans switched their allegiance, rooting for Koufax to strike out Harry Bright as long shadows painted the diamond, and break the World Series single-game record of 14 strikeouts. He did. A few thousand Dodgers fans, having refused to quit on their team even after the move west, exulted. Thousands more Yankee fans sulked into the subways.

After that opening win, Dodgers coach Leo (The Lip) Durocher approached Podres:

"That's a pretty hard act to follow."

Johnny said: "You watch me."

Winners of 104 games, the 1963 Yankees belted 188 home runs, despite injuries to Mantle and Maris. The Yankees won the World Series in two of the previous three years, beating the San Francisco Giants in 1962 and the Cincinnati Reds in 1961, and barely losing to the Pittsburgh Pirates in 1960, on Bill Mazeroski's ninth-inning walk-off home run in Game Seven.

The Dodgers won 99 games and boasted the best pitching staff in baseball, with a team earned-run average of 2.85, 24 shutouts and 1,095 strikeouts. Sandy Koufax won the Cy Young and National League Most Valuable Player awards with a 25-5 record, 1.88 ERA, 11 shutouts, and 306 strikeouts. Don Drysdale went 19-17 with a 2.63 ERA.

Podres won 14 and lost 12, with a 3.54 ERA and five shutouts (fifth best in the National League). Ron Perranoski, in his greatest season, anchored the bullpen with a 16-3 record, 1.67 ERA, and 21 saves, leading the league in appearances and winning percentage and finishing fourth in the voting for National League MVP. With pitching and speed as the team strengths, the Dodgers scored only 640 runs, a considerable decline from 842 in 1962. Despite a lightweight .357 team slugging percentage and only 110 homers, a few of the hitters performed brilliantly.

Tommy Davis won his second straight batting title with a .326 average. Maury Wills hit .302 with 40 stolen bases, and Ron Fairly contributed 12 homers and a .347 on-base percentage. Frank "Hondo" Howard slugged at a .518 pace with 28 round trippers. In one of the most memorable moments of the first game of the World Series, Howard belted a low line drive that zipped by Mantle, blazed past the center field monuments, then on the playing field, and short-hopped the wall at the 476-foot mark. Bleacherites in the $1.50 day-of-the-game seats were ready to duck to avoid being hit with what looked like a mortar shot. Partly because of the speed of the rebound back to Mantle and partly because Howard was slow afoot, it went only for a double. "It looked like it was hit with a two-iron," recalled Podres, who saw it from the dugout.

The winner of 13 games against only 5 defeats, Downing struck out 171 batters in just over 175 innings, compiling a 2.56 ERA. He yielded only seven home runs (compared to 26 given up by "The Chairman of the Board," Whitey Ford). Later in his career, Downing would become a Dodger, winning 20 games in 1971 and gaining immortality on April 8, 1974, as the victim of Hank Aaron's 715th home run. But before this game, Yankees manager Ralph Houk praised Downing to the *Los Angeles Times*.

"Downing has all the pitches and is faster than most hurlers in our league. And I can assure you that base runners don't get much of a jump on this kid."

In the top of the first inning, leadoff batter Maury Wills tested Houk's theories after lashing a single past the pitcher. Before Downing could deliver his second pitch to the next batter, Jim Gilliam, Wills took off, and Downing rifled the ball to first baseman Joe Pepitone. Without a second thought, Wills continued racing toward second. Pepitone's throw pulled Bobby Richardson toward shortstop and Wills dove, grabbing the bag. Safe!

"I don't think Wills was fooled by my motion," Downing said later. "I think the hit and run was probably on. I was just trying to hold him close." Today, Downing remembers, "Wills was able to beat the throw by using a great hook slide!" But Richardson recalls the incident differently. "I ran in front of Tony Kubek to receive the throw from first and my momentum kept me going and allowed Maury to be safe. If I had let Kubek take it, it would have been an easy play and Maury would have been out."

With Downing already unnerved, the Dodgers continued to attack. Downing threw three straight balls to Gilliam, before he singled sharply to right. Wills rounded third, bluffing a dash home, and Maris threw to the plate, without a cutoff. Maury returned to third while Gilliam adroitly took second on the throw. Willie Davis, the "man of a thousand stances," stepped to the plate. Copying Stan Musial on the advice of the scout who signed him, Kenny Myers, Davis smashed Downing's fastball towards Maris, who failed to pick up the flight of the ball and slipped and fell to his knees. The ball bounced to the wall in right field, a two-run double.

Davis thought for a moment that his double would be a sacrifice fly. "But the ball was hit better than Maris thought," he said later. "He started in on it, then stumbled trying to go back. But I think it would have scored one run even if he caught it."

Now it was Podres' turn on the mound, staked to a 2-0 lead. Before the game, a *Los Angeles Times* reporter asked him, "What do you think of the heralded Yankee power?"

"I'll stick their bats in their ears!"

Confidence and a positive attitude pumped Johnny for a crucial game. In his last start of the regular season on September 29th, Johnny lost to the Phillies and Dennis Bennett, 12-3.

"I still remember my final start of the season against Philadelphia. It was a tune-up for the World Series and I gave up eight runs (in one and two-thirds innings). But Walter Alston told Drysdale that he had to have another lefty pitch at Yankee Stadium, so I got the start."

Podres retired leadoff batter Tony Kubek and the next batter, Richardson. Tom Tresh then singled to left field on the first pitch. Mickey Mantle hit a long drive to right center but Frank Howard made a sensational, leaping, one-handed catch to end the inning, and Mantle threw his helmet in disgust.

In the second, Yankees catcher Elston Howard reached first on an infield single knocked down by Dick Tracewski. Podres walked Pepitone, but before the Yankees could mount a rally, Johnny struck out Clete Boyer, then Downing to end the threat.

With two out in the Dodgers' third, Tommy Davis hit one of Downing's pitches into the right-field corner. Trying to field the ball, Maris ran into the wall. Davis wound up on third base, and Maris was led off the field with a bruised arm, finishing him for the Series. Bill (Moose) Skowron, acquired from the Yankees in an off-season trade for pitcher Stan Williams, stepped to the plate. During the season, Skowron was a major disappointment, batting only .203 in 89 games, with four homers, 19 RBIs, and a woeful .287 slugging percentage. In his previous three seasons with the Yankees, the slugger hit 77 home runs. This time, he sliced the ball down the right-field line (his favorite target while a Yankee) for a home run, and the Dodgers led 3-0. According to Skowron, "The pitch came in outside and I went with it. It was a bad pitch, but when I'm going good I hit pitches like that."

Now the Yankees saw vintage Podres. Johnny retired 13 consecutive batters before Tresh (who had homered against Koufax the day before) singled with one out in the sixth. Tresh went to second when Podres' pickoff attempt missed Skowron for an error. Several spectators then ran onto the field but were removed and play was resumed, with Mickey Mantle at the plate. Mantle sent a Podres' pitch to deep center, but speedster Willie Davis ran it down for the final out.

By the sixth inning, Downing was gone, relieved by Ralph Terry, matching the MVP of the '62 Series with the MVP of the '55 Series. The Yankee Stadium lights went on in the seventh inning as rain began falling. Intermittent drizzle continued until the ninth. In the middle of the seventh, Stadium public address announcer Bob Sheppard (who began his long career as a broadcaster for the Brooklyn Dodgers football team) informed the fans in his deep, serious, monotone, that tickets would soon go on sale for Games Six and Seven. Derisive laughter, doubtless from giddy Dodgers fans, sprinkled throughout the crowd. Then, in the eighth inning, Willie Davis drilled a double to right off Terry and quickly came home on a triple by his roommate (but not his relative), Tommy Davis, to make it 4-0. Tommy's second triple tied a World Series record.

Johnny Podres

In the ninth, Podres talked briefly with pitching coach Joe Becker before preparing to face Mantle for the fourth time. Mantle hit yet another long drive, but Tommy Davis was waiting for it in left center near the warning track. Rounding first, Mantle kicked the dirt, evoking memories of Joe DiMaggio's reaction to Dodger Al Gionfriddo's famous catch in the 1947 World Series. As Mantle wandered toward the dugout, Yankee failure seemed certain.

With one out, Podres faced Hector Lopez, who replaced the injured Maris in the third inning and had already swatted a double off Podres. Podres threw Lopez a slow curve that sprang from a quick motion. Lopez blooped the ball over Jim Gilliam's head, down the left-field line and into the stands for a ground-rule double. Now a coach in the Yankees' minor league system, Lopez recalled that the pitch was indeed a breaking ball and that Podres was "a very smart pitcher who threw a lot of strikes and kept you off balance."

With Lopez standing at second, Alston ran out to the mound. "Are you okay, John?" Alston inquired. Podres remembered the exchange:

"'Yeah skip, I'm alright, I feel good,' I told him. But Alston asked me again, 'You sure you're all right? I've got Perry (Perranoski) ready.'

"And about the third time he asked me, I said, 'Walt, are you trying to tell me that you want to bring Perry in the game?' He said 'yeah.' So I said, 'What are you waiting for? Bring the son of a bitch in.'"

Alston, who noticed that Podres was breathing heavily, later said that he "hated to take Podres out when he had the shutout going and probably would have wound up getting the side out anyway."

But Alston made his decision to relieve him and Podres heard cheers from the Yankee Stadium crowd as he walked back to the Dodger dugout. It was Johnny's last appearance in a World Series Game. He told the *Los Angeles Times* afterward: "Sure I'd like another shutout but there's no sense fooling myself when we've got the greatest relief pitcher in baseball."

The first man to face Perranoski was catcher Elston Howard, the American League Most Valuable Player (and the Yankees' best hitter during 1963). Howard promptly singled to right center and Lopez scored, spoiling the shutout. The run was charged to Podres, even though "the greatest relief pitcher" let it in, and ended John's streak of 19 scoreless innings against the Yankees in World Series play. Podres pitched 8 1/3 innings of one-run ball, scattered six hits (no more than one per inning), struck out four and walked only one, and collected a single. His pitch repertoire included 75 fastballs (50 for strikes), and 18 curveballs.

Perranoski was worried about his control after not having pitched in a week, but after Howard's at-bat, he recalled, "My control came back and I felt comfortable." He got Joe Pepitone to ground into a force play and struck out third baseman Clete Boyer to end the game, securing the Dodgers' 2-0 series advantage as they headed to Los Angeles.

"I'm really glad that he brought Perry in because as it turned out, he was our only reliever to pitch in the series," Podres said. "It was great that he got the chance. As long as we won the series, that was fine with me."

In just two hours and thirteen minutes, Game Two was history. Tommy and Willie Davis shook hands in the Dodger clubhouse. "What do you say, Baby?" Tommy asked Willie.

"I say goodbye, New York. We won't be back!"

Interviewed after the game, Podres adopted a more modest stance toward his Yankee foes: "Mantle probably would have had three home runs today if we had been playing this game in Dodger Stadium. Mickey didn't get any hits off me but he hit me real good." Mantle told the *New York Times*: "Podres looked just the way he did last time I faced him in the Series. We thought he would tire about the sixth inning but he didn't. He knows how to pitch. He is not as fast as Sandy Koufax but he's just as good."

"I didn't have real good rhythm at the start, and I was probably a little nervous," Podres said. "But after awhile I got my feet on the ground. The fellows made some outstanding plays behind me, and those early runs really helped."

Al Downing remembered: "Podres pitched an outstanding game and, more important, held our right-handed hitters in check!"

On October 4, 1963, the *Los Angeles Times* headline trumpeted: "Podres Cracks Whip, Yanks Jump, 4-1." The *New York Times* headline ran: "Witherbee's Hero Does It Again—Podres Overcomes Short Fences and an Aching Back."

According to the *Los Angeles Times*, "Podres couldn't quite make it all the way Thursday. The last time [he faced the Yankees] he was only 23. The eight years had taken their toll and the strength and stamina were not quite there to finish it up." Yet, "Podres again displayed the class and courage with which he beat the Yankees in 1955 to sweep the Dodgers to their first world championship."

Jim Murray wrote in his *Los Angeles Times* column: "John Podres that celebrated bon vivant, marriage counselor (he counsels against it), and woodcraft instructor expertly stuffed the Yankee bats into their hip pockets. John ran his finger down the Yankee lineup and decided he wouldn't even have to go to bed early to beat these guys."

Johnny also told the press that Drysdale and Koufax would beat the Yankees in Los Angeles to sweep the series. That made Koufax and

Johnny Podres

Drysdale a little uneasy. But when the series shifted to Dodger Stadium, Don Drysdale shut out the Yankees 1-0 in Game Three, a pitching duel with Jim Bouton. In the first inning, Tommy Davis singled to drive in Jim Gilliam for the game's only run.

Game Four was a rematch between Koufax and Whitey Ford. The Dodgers collected only two hits, a single and a home run by Frank Howard, and scored another run on a sacrifice fly by Willie Davis. Koufax yielded only one run, a home run by Mickey Mantle in the seventh inning, and gained a complete-game 2-1 victory.

For the series, Koufax, Drysdale, Podres and Perranoski combined for an earned run average of 1.00, holding the Yankees to four runs, a .171 batting average and five walks. They recorded 37 strikeouts. The Dodgers won with a team batting average of just .214. There was no question about it. Good pitching beat good hitting.

Podres' achievements in the Fall Classic, more than 40 years later, remain tops among Dodgers pitchers. He is tied with Sandy Koufax as the all-time Brooklyn and Los Angeles Dodger leader in World Series victories (Koufax, however, lost three World Series games—in 1959, 1965 and 1966).

In six World Series games, Podres won four and lost only one; threw 38 1/3 innings, with 18 strikeouts, one shutout and two complete games. He compiled a 2.11 earned run average. Johnny also batted .312 in series play, including a double and an RBI.

The four-game sweep of the Yankees ranks as the greatest achievement in the history of the Los Angeles Dodgers, just as 1955 was the greatest year ever for the Brooklyn Dodgers. The L.A. Dodgers beat the Yankees in four straight games (after losing the first two) to win the 1981 World Series. Kirk Gibson's home run off Dennis Eckersley in 1988 qualifies as one of the great moments in World Series history. But nothing can compare to a four-game sweep of the Yankees by the Men in Blue.

Podres put it this way then and four decades later, "When you played in the World Series, you always wanted to beat the best and we beat the best. It was always a thrill to beat the Yankees."

No Dodger did it better.

Bob, John and Robert S. Bennett

Box Score - October 3, 1963, Game Two of the World Series, Dodgers 4, Yankees 1.

LOS ANGELES (NL)	AB	R	H	RBI	NEW YORK (AL)	AB	R	H	RBI
Wills, ss	4	1	2	0	Kubek, ss	4	0	0	0
Gilliam, 3b	4	1	1	0	Richardson, 2b	4	0	1	0
W. Davis, cf	4	1	1	2	Tresh, lf	4	0	2	0
T. Davis, lf	4	0	2	1	Mantle, cf	4	0	0	0
F. Howard, rf	3	0	0	0	Maris, rf	1	0	0	0
Fairly, rf	0	0	0	0	Lopez, rf	3	1	2	0
Skowron, 1b	4	1	2	1	E. Howard, c	4	0	2	1
Tracewski, 2b	3	0	0	0	Pepitone, 1b	3	0	0	0
Roseboro, c	4	0	0	0	Boyer, 3b	4	0	0	0
Podres, p	4	0	1	0	Downing, p	1	0	0	0
Perranoski, p	0	0	0	0	Bright, ph	1	0	0	0
					Terry, p	0	0	0	0
Total:	34	4	10	4	Linz, ph	1	0	0	0
					Reniff, p	0	0	0	0
					Total:	34	1	7	1

```
Los Angeles Dodgers   2 0 0 1 0 0 0 1 0 -- 4
New York Yankees      0 0 0 0 0 0 0 0 1 -- 1
```

Error: Podres. Left on Base: Los Angeles 5, New York 7. 2B: W. Davis 2, Lopez 2. 3B: T. Davis 2. HR: Skowron (1), 4th inning off Downing. SB: Wills.

	IP	H	R	ER	BB	SO	ERA
Podres (W, 1-0)	8 1/3	6	1	1	1	4	1.08
Perranoski	2/3	1	0	0	0	1	0.00
Downing (L, 0-1)	5	7	3	3	1	6	5.40
Terry	3	3	1	1	1	0	3.00
Reniff	1	0	0	0	0	0	0.00

Umpires: Gorman (NL), home; Napp (AL), first base; Crawford (NL), second base; Paparella (AL), third base; Venzon (NL), left field; Rice (AL), right field. Time of game: 2:13. Attendance: 66,455.

Chapter Three
Just Like His Father

John Joseph Podres arrived safe at home just in time for major league baseball post-season play, September 30, 1932. He was the first of four boys and a girl born to Joseph and Anna Podres of Witherbee, New York, a valley village between Lake Champlain and the Adirondack Mountains. His father mined iron in nearby Mineville, the source of the magnets used 100 years earlier in the invention of the electric motor by a Vermont blacksmith, Thomas Davenport. Joe Podres also threw baseballs.

"I grew up like any other kid in a small town in the North Country," Johnny recalls. "I hoed the potatoes and chopped the kindling wood to start the fire in the coal stove." He also put a radio under his pillow on spring and summer nights when Dodgers announcers Red Barber and Connie Desmond described the feats of his heroes, who included Gil Hodges, Jackie Robinson, Carl Furillo and Pee Wee Reese.

"Their voices were so familiar it was like they were members of the family.

"I'll never forget when, late at night, Barber would say 'F.O.B.,' the bases are full of Brooks. That might happen just when my father would tell me to shut the radio off because I had to go to school the next day.

"As a kid in school, I wanted to be a Dodger. I was a Dodgers fan. I loved the Dodgers. In those days every little town had a semi-pro team that played on Sundays. People would sit in their cars and blow their horns for a big hit, a strikeout or a good play. They had tailgate parties long before they became fashionable at NFL football games. My dad was the pitcher, and I went to all the games from about the time I was old enough to walk. I always wanted to be like my father. I wanted to be a pitcher.

"Sometimes somebody would hit a ball into the woods and I would find it and hide it and then we kids would choose up sides and play in a cow pasture and use cow patties for bases. You wouldn't want to slide into some of them. Some balls that were hit you wouldn't want to catch on a bounce."

In a small town sometimes it's difficult to round up enough youngsters to play a game, so then Johnny would throw by himself, sometimes a ball, and sometimes rocks. "A lot of us kids were good at throwing rocks—we had a lot of rock fights, too."

The North Country produces comparatively few ballplayers, but when a good one emerges, he is likely to be a pitcher. The climate makes you handier with a snowball than a baseball bat.

"I guess my father had me throwing a baseball starting when I was about six. He was a fine pitcher and many people in the area thought his stuff was good enough for the majors if he hadn't been mining ore to keep our family in the necessities of life. He had a great 'drop,' which is what everybody used to call an over-the-top curveball—one that 'falls off the table'. Once while working at the mine he fell 40 feet off a bluff, did a somersault in the air and landed on his feet and broke both legs. But he still pitched after that."

One day while playing catch with his father, Johnny began to imitate all sorts of southpaw pitching motions. Youngster Benny Butinski, standing nearby, said, "There's Elmer the Great." For years wherever Johnny went—Witherbee, Mineville, Moriah or Port Henry—6,000 people within a six-mile radius called him Elmer.

They also affectionately called him "Honey Boy," because of his lack of jealousy, his fairness and good sportsmanship as evidenced from early boyhood.

At the age of 12, Johnny decided to become a pole-vaulter, but used a tamping stick, employed by miners, in the absence of a regulation pole. Tamping sticks don't have the girth of a real vaulting pole and Johnny's snapped one day at an altitude of 11 feet. He landed flat on his back in pain. He nevertheless continued to vault and later did well in the event at Mineville High School. He was captain of the basketball team there, too.

The tamping stick and high school vaulting put a cramp in more than his back. They plagued his pitching career for years. His condition, diagnosed as spondylosis, wore him down in the second half of several seasons later on in the majors. After first-half fast starts, he often suffered several losses as the season wore on. His chronic ailment forced him to sleep with a board under his mattress.

"I really don't know when I hurt my back, but I have a sneaking hunch I did it when I used to pole vault in high school. Maybe I jarred something when I landed in the pit." He told a *Los Angeles Times* reporter years later, "There are times when I feel like I've never had a sore back, and then there are times when it stiffens so much that my roomie has to tie my shoe laces for me."

As a high school hurler, beginning as a freshman, he lost only three games in four years. "Of course, we only played about eight games every spring because it was so cold, or snowy, or raining and the next thing you knew school got out," he said. When he wasn't pitching, he played the outfield and often hit home runs. During the summers, lacking any other organized ball in the area, Johnny pitched for a town team and recalls once pitching a game against his father but can't remember who won.

Johnny credits four people with helping his early career—his father, Mineville High coach Steve Kazlo, Princeton University assistant baseball coach Matt Davidson, who spent summers in Witherbee, and Mineville principal William Dwyer, who knew several big-league scouts.

"I put Johnny in Prof. Dwyer's hands," Joseph Podres told a reporter back then. "He was the one who got the scouts interested. We weren't shopping for the best offer; we were looking for advice. The professor insisted that if Johnny couldn't make the big leagues soon after 1950 (the year he was graduated from high school) he must go to college."

"Scouts from Brooklyn, Cincinnati, the Phillies, the Yankees, St. Louis Browns, Detroit and the Boston Red Sox looked at him," Dwyer said. "We liked George Sisler's approach. He was Brooklyn's head scout. He was going to give his honest opinion as to whether Johnny should sign or go to college. He didn't want him to be a baseball bum." Before Sisler, until 2004 the all-time single season hit leader, got a look at him at Ebbets Field, Dodgers scout Alex Isabel gave Johnny a new glove and then watched as he threw a no-hitter for Mineville High. He came back a second time and Johnny threw another no-hitter.

When Sisler saw him pitch at Ebbets Field, he said, "Don't let that kid get away. We'll give him $6,000 for the first year. He'll be in the big leagues in four years."

After hearing that, the kid he was spent the last $5 in his pocket taking amusement park rides at nearby Coney Island. But he didn't make the big club in four years. He made it in two.

The July after high school graduation Johnny pitched for Valley Field, Quebec, located a couple of hours north of Witherbee. In August he went across Lake Champlain to the Burlington, Vermont, Cardinals in the (old, independent Class D) Northern League, whose alumni also included the Phillies' great pitchers Curt Simmons and Robin Roberts. Clary Anderson managed the Cardinals then and later had an outstanding career as a high school and college coach and wrote a good book of baseball instruction for youngsters. Both of Johnny's teams that summer were the equivalent of today's Single-A caliber. By the end of the summer of 1950 he had signed with the Dodgers.

"When I had a chance to sign with them, that's what I wanted to do. It's not often you get a chance to play for your favorite team. I always wanted to be a Dodger.

"About that $6,000 bonus, it was really only $5,200. The other $800 was my salary for '51-- $160 a month for five months."

Everybody who knew Podres' parents called them an outstanding example of American parenthood. While the father won the bread the hard way in mining, the mother kept an immaculate home and both kept close to and had the confidence of their children. Johnny loved Witherbee and lived there all of his 18 years before becoming a professional. He returned home to the town of about 1,800 year after year.

"A small town," he says, "is the only place to live. I love Witherbee. I can find more friends there than in the rest of the world." An avid fisherman, Johnny enjoys the Adirondack Mountain trout streams and ponds and Lake Champlain, and even now, in his seventies, can be found with a rod in the summer and in a "shanty" on the ice of the big lake in winter.

"The nights were always quiet in Witherbee. It's beautiful country; just beautiful."

Joseph Podres backed Johnny's budding career. In 1950, he often drove his son over a Lake Champlain bridge to pitch for the Burlington Cardinals' Vermont games. In 1952, when Johnny moved up to the Montreal Royals, the AAA Dodgers affiliate in the International League, his father watched from the stands because the Quebec ball park was only a couple of hours north of Witherbee. Both his father and mother attended big league games Johnny pitched at Ebbets Field and in the Polo Grounds.

"One night my mother was in the Polo Grounds where we were playing the Mets before they finished building Shea Stadium. She watched me strike out 14."

His father, two uncles and a contingent of co-workers from the iron mine were at Yankee Stadium when Johnny shut out the Yankees in the seventh game of the 1955 World Series. Dodgers reliever Ed Roebuck said what he remembered most about that Series was the relationship between Johnny and his father.

Johnny Podres

"In the clubhouse after Johnny pitched the shutout to win the final game," Roebuck said, "they were hugging and crying."

Work and distance kept his dad home in Witherbee in 1951 when Johnny pitched for Newport News, Virginia, in the old Piedmont League and at Hazard, Kentucky, in the Mountain State League. At Newport News for only an unimpressive month, he was sent down to Hazard on May 15. By the beginning of September he compiled a record of 21-3, with 228 strikeouts in 200 innings and a 1.67 earned run average, tops in the league in all three categories. The mayor of the town presented him with a bronze plaque after that season, proclaiming Johnny an official "Duke of Hazard." It still hangs on his family room wall. And the governor made him an honest-to-goodness "Kentucky Colonel."

"You never would have bet on that record if you saw the first game I pitched in Hazard," he recalled. "It was a Sunday afternoon and I gave up seven runs in the first inning. So many hard shots were hit to the left side of the infield that my manager, who also played first base, hollered out, 'Give the third baseman a mask and a chest protector'. I said to myself, 'Boy, where do we go from here?' But I shut them out the rest of the way and we ended up winning the game 14-7.

"After the season I needed a job and landed one with Republic Steel in Witherbee. I wasn't crazy about going to work in the mines but I kept pestering them and finally they gave me a job on the surface in one of the mills. If I hadn't been a ballplayer I probably would have had to go into the mines, like most of my friends."

Because of the outstanding performance at Hazard, the Dodgers promoted him to the Triple-A Montreal club in '52. At Montreal, he pitched 88 innings in 24 games and wound up with a 5-5 record and a 3.27 earned run average, collecting 47 strikeouts, giving up 76 hits and issuing 39 bases on balls.

"I didn't have a real good spring in '53, but I made the big club. I was in the right place at the right time, when the Dodgers really needed left-handed pitching."

On August 12, 1961, Johnny was 18-5 and well on his way to his first 20-game-winning season when Joseph Podres became gravely ill. Johnny left the team to be at his dad's bedside in a Burlington, Vermont, hospital, the largest one near Witherbee. His father died in September at only 51 years of age. Johnny's mother, at this writing, is 95 and still lives in Witherbee in the house where he was born.

Johnny married Joan Taylor of Ardmore, Pennsylvania, in 1966. They have two sons, Joseph and John. Two years earlier, the romance had an icy beginning.

Bob, John and Robert S. Bennett

"I was staying in a hotel in Los Angeles," Johnny said. "I had a room that looked down on the swimming pool and when I saw her sunbathing down there, I poured a pitcher of ice water out the window right on her back. So then I went down and apologized and introduced myself. At first she didn't believe me when I told her I pitched for the Dodgers.

"She was a skater with Shipstad's and Johnston's Ice Follies which toured the country and was performing in LA then. She had about the same kind of life as a ballplayer. We both traveled the country to various cities to perform. So for the next couple of years it was long-distance dating."

Johnny and Joan live just "down the road apiece" from Witherbee in Queensbury, New York.

Chapter Four
Three Years on the Big Club

Just 18 years old, his first year out of high school, Johnny reported to Dodgertown in Vero Beach, Florida, in the spring of 1951, joining his boyhood diamond heroes.

"There I was with Robinson, Reese, Snider and Newcombe and the rest of them. It was unbelievable!"

Most had played together for several years in those days before free agency made many major leaguers into nomadic hired guns. Just about anybody paying attention could predict the starting lineup every spring for about 10 years in a row. They were a team when teammates stuck together for the long haul. In fact, several regulars were well into their thirties. They won six pennants over 10 years, the first of them when Jackie Robinson joined in 1947, becoming the first black ballplayer in the majors.

After an outstanding 1951 season in Class D, the next spring Johnny left Vero Beach and jumped to the Triple-A International League Montreal Royals. When the Dodgers broke for the north after 1953 Dodgertown training, Johnny joined the big club for good.

The '53 regular season became the best by the storied, actual "Boys of Summer." Much has been written about the starting lineup of Junior Gilliam, Gil Hodges, Reese, Robinson, Billy Cox, Campanella, Snider and Carl Furillo. The team produced a major-league record 208 home runs. Campanella drove home a club record 142 runs and won his second MVP trophy. Five of the regulars hit better than .300. Furillo won the batting crown at .344 and Gilliam picked up the Rookie of the Year award. Six players scored more than 100 runs and three drove in more than 100.

Altogether, this team topped every other in the majors in homers, batting and slugging average, runs scored, stolen bases and fielding percentage. The Dodgers piled up 105 wins against just 49 losses, their best record ever.

Veterans Erskine, Russ Meyer, Loes, Roe and Labine led the pitching staff. Newcombe was in the Army. Besides Podres, just 20 years old, Roe, at 38, was the only lefty on the staff, including the relief corps. The rookie Podres compiled a record of 9-4, with a winning percentage of .692, fourth best on the roster that included 14 hurlers over the course of the season. He started 18 games, pitched 115 innings, struck out 82 and walked 64, allowing 126 hits. His earned run average of 4.23 was bested only by Erskine's 3.53 among the regular starters. Podres was among five pitchers with a shutout.

Johnny claimed his first major league victory on May 24. He entered a 2-2 game at Philadelphia in the fifth inning in relief of Jim Hughes, who put two Phillies on base with no outs. Podres prevented them from scoring and the Dodgers scored a go-ahead run in the sixth, when the pitcher left for a pinch hitter. They added a then-record dozen in the eighth and another in the ninth for a 16-2 victory.

On October 5, Johnny, just 21 years and five days old, became the second youngest pitcher to start a World Series game. In the third inning, the Yankees' Joe Collins hit a drive that bounced off the heel of first baseman Gil Hodges' glove for an error. It would have been the third out of three scoreless innings. But then Johnny hit Hank Bauer and walked Yogi Berra. Dressen decided to bring in Russ Meyer, who promptly served up a grand slam to Mickey Mantle, a blow that won the game and pinned the first Fall Classic defeat on Johnny. It would be the last.

Glenn Mickens was a right-handed reliever with the Dodgers in '53 who later became a baseball coach at UCLA for 35 years. Among the major league players he coached in college were Chris Chambliss, Mike Gallego, Don Slaught, Todd Zeile, Eric Karros and Jeff Conine. He now lives in Hawaii.

"It was a pleasure," Mickens told us, "to be with Johnny in those Vero Beach days and briefly in 1953. Johnny was the best competitive left-handed pitcher I ever played with. He was a no-nonsense, give-me-the-ball pitcher and a manager's dream. If you were going to beat John you were going to beat him with his best pitch—not his second or third best.

"The Dodgers taught all their pitchers the 'pull the shade' changeup and no one mastered that pitch better than John. The first batter Charlie Dressen brought me in to face in relief, after I was called up from Fort Worth, was Ted Kluszewski of Cincinnati. He had arms bigger than my

Johnny Podres

legs and all I didn't want him to do was hit it up the middle! I got a couple of strikes on him, got a fast ball 'away' and he hit a rope that tore up three box seats in left center field.

"When I came back to the dugout in shock, Podres was laughing and said, 'Mick, he's hit four or five off me and I throw from the left side. Don't feel bad!'"

After that, Kluszewski said the pitchers made him into a home run hitter. "When I came up I was a spray hitter. The pitchers forced me into hitting home runs. It was self-preservation for the pitchers. I was hitting a lot of line drives through the box. So they started coming inside. Well, if you adjust correctly you have to pull the ball and when you pull the ball you just necessarily hit more home runs."

It was a great season but the last for Dressen at the helm, however. He had won two pennants after just missing in '51 and sought a long-term contract from owner Walter O'Malley. The king of one-year contracts, O'Malley fired him after the season and hired Walter Alston, who skippered the team for 23 years. On 23 one-year contracts.

But Podres remained a fan of Dressen.

"Charlie was the one who brought me up to the big club, and he taught me the change-up," Podres recalls. That change-up was widely regarded as the best in the majors and reliever Mickens reminded recently that "Johnny proved it in the '55 Series." Alston called it a "change-up on his curve."

His change-up, the curve and a varied velocity of other pitches brought Johnny adjectives from sportswriters that included stylish, crafty, gritty, smart, professional and even brilliant.

Over the years his pitching contemporaries included such luminaries as Newcombe, Erskine, Koufax, Drysdale and Sutton, some of the best the game has ever known. His statistics say a lot, but those who really knew Johnny said he was a "money pitcher." They meant that he was the big-game pitcher, or simply the guy you wanted on the mound no matter how many other flashy hurlers you might have, when you *absolutely* needed a win. His general manager, Buzzie Bavasi, made sure we knew that's how he regarded Johnny most of all.

Los Angeles Times columnist Jim Murray put it this way: "He'll beat the Yanks for you, but the Mets might put him in the shower."

Former Cincinnati pitcher Jim Brosnan, in his baseball book, *The Long Season*, called Johnny "the only pro on the staff. When he's got his stuff, lock up and go home." Reese was fond of saying, "When Johnny had his stuff, he could pitch in a telephone booth."

Catcher Joe Pignatano recently recalled the Podres big curve and change-up: "You could catch them with tweezers." His change-up was also described as a pitch that came to the plate like a feather on a bubble while his fastball wore a hole in Roy Campanella's mitt.

Those were not isolated observations. One opposing manager said, "When John Podres has his stuff, you feel like carrying a white handkerchief to home plate by the third inning." Columnist Murray wrote, "Podres' pitching style is modeled after a man with a shell game. The ball comes out of a welter of legs, arms ands head movements at such different speeds that a man with instructions to take the pitch can get dizzy and wonder how many he's taken."

The Braves' Johnny Logan once said, "I get the feeling Podres has spit the ball at me."

"He squirts the ball out of his tentacles like an octopus," another said.

"When Johnny has his law-breaking stuff, the batter gets the sensation he's rolling it to them," Campanella observed.

Casey Stengel called Podres a "professional pitcher, who throws a fast ball, a curve, a change-up and if they hit it, he stuffs his glove in his pocket and heads for the shower. When he's got his stuff, Mickey Mantle looks like Larry Burright (a light-hitting Dodgers utility infielder)."

In 1954, Johnny emerged as the leading lefty on the team. He compiled a record of 11 and 3 with two shutouts, but then required an appendectomy in mid-season and lost his last four decisions. He started 21 games, completing six. He allowed 147 hits in 152 innings, struck out 79 and walked 53, with a 4.26 earned run average. Fellow lefties, Roe, and the star-crossed Karl Spooner, won only three and two, respectively.

In the fateful year of '55, Johnny had solidified his place on the squad, even though at 22, "I was the youngest guy on the club except for Koufax," he reminisced at his kitchen table. Then he recalled his teammates that year.

Dodgers Pitchers in '55

"In '53 and '54 I always wanted to hang around Preacher Roe to get some pointers about pitching.

"Unless the guy was known as a first-ball swinger, Roe told me, one of those who would swing at a horse apple, try to get that first pitch over. Try to get ahead of the hitter. He also taught me how to play poker. But he was 39 in '54 and gone in '55. That meant the left-handers were Spooner, Sandy Koufax and me.

"Spooner was unbelievable. In '54 he pitched two shutouts, and struck out 27 in two games, but he had arm problems. In '55 he was 8-6 but after that he was gone because of his arm. I remember he had relieved me without really being warmed up. Years later, Don Drysdale and I went to visit him when he was tending bar in Florida. Don and I were having a loud conversation, with a lot of swear words, and Karl kicked us out!

"Koufax was the best pitcher I ever saw, bar none. In Brooklyn, though, he would strike out 14 or 15 and then throw two or three to the backstop. He was only 19 in '54 and he pitched only 42 innings and went two and two. Remember, he was a 'bonus baby' and with the rules they had then they couldn't send him down to the minors where he could get some experience so he mostly sat on the bench. But once he got it together there was nobody better.

"I never saw a guy with such a smooth delivery and boy did he put everything into it. I joined the Dodgers a year ahead of him and when he got there he was just a wild, hard-throwing left-hander. It took him about five years but he finally turned it around. I think the Dodgers were getting ready to give up on him, but then overnight he put it all together and for the next five or six years he was the best pitcher I saw. He became a perfectionist out there.

"Erskine, who won a lot of games for Brooklyn, saved the first game I pitched. He was 28 in '55 and only Newcombe was older, among the starters. Carl won 11 games for us that year.

"Newk was really nice to watch pitch, but he could also hit and play first base. He was a big left-handed batter but was a right-handed pitcher. He went 20 and 5 and certainly was the ace of the staff. I remember Newk would run and run before a game and he would really sweat and he told me he was sweating out the booze from the night before. I had heard him talking about being an alcoholic and I told him I never saw him drink much. 'You're white and I'm black,' he told me 'and after the game you go your way and I go mine. I used to drink a bottle every night.'

"Billy Loes was dumb like a fox. That guy knew every hitter by heart. I used to ask him for advice on how to pitch to different guys. He was really astute. He's in Arizona now. He drove a hack for awhile in New York. We used to play poker and when he started blinking I turned over my cards. He won 10 games for us that year.

"I would like to see Clem Labine pitch every day today for one inning at a time the way these relievers do now, because he had a great curve. He was a starter though and went 13-6 in '55. Later on when we were in Los Angeles we shared a two-room apartment. We agreed that if one of us got traded, all the stuff we bought for it, the sheets, blankets, pillows, dishes and pots and pans, would stay with the apartment. A month later he got traded to Detroit. I went to Buzzie (Bavasi, the general manager) and said

'You traded my roommate,' so Buzzie paid half of the rent for the rest of that season. I also remember that before Clem left we got a couple of eviction notices. We had some pretty good parties there.

The Lineup

"Campy used to sit on the bench, all by himself, getting ready to catch, and think about how he was going to work the hitters. He was unbelievable. One time Dressen called a meeting to change Campy's signs, because opposing players on second base were relaying his signs to their bench, where they were trying to figure out a pattern. But Campy always kept them puzzled, sometimes using an extra finger. I won't tell you which one but he pointed it up instead of down.

"Behind the plate, he would sit outside and you could throw it off the corner and get the call. He was the best I ever saw at keeping the ball in front of him. He didn't have the strongest arm but threw out runners because he got rid of it faster than the best of them. Campy kept the game moving and the umpires liked that. If you had a five-run lead and the wind was blowing in on a nice day in Chicago, where they only played day games then, you could throw it off the plate to Campy. The ump would call just about anything a strike to get the game over.

"Gil, at first base, was a great team guy—an every day strong guy. Sometimes when he would get in one of his slumps, Alston would be furious. Pitchers could throw him inside and he would swing and miss. Then they would throw him outside and he'd take it for a called strike. So then all the priests and ministers and rabbis in Brooklyn would ask the people to pray for Gil. And pretty soon he would get some big hits.

"Robinson might go oh for four, two or three days in a row but he would run around and shake everybody's hand when we won without him hitting. When Jackie got older, and he was 36 in '55, he had spurts where he played like he was a 20-year-old kid. I remember one day in Chicago when he reached first and told their pitcher, Sam Jones, 'I'm stealing second and third' and he did."

His friendship with Don (Popeye) Zimmer, a utility infielder who later managed and still coached in 2004, goes back to '54. "He took me out to Belmont Park, and introduced me to the horse track. I won $120 that day and I told him 'Popeye, this is easy money.' Then we went out again the next day and I won $100 more. Since then I think it has cost me a million."

The phone rang, as it often does in the Podres kitchen. Likely as not, it's one of his old pals and this time, as luck would have it, it was Zimmer

Johnny Podres

himself. He had a few days off because he didn't have to make the trip to the West Coast with his team, the Tampa Bay Devil Rays, which he coached.

"Yeah," Johnny told him, "I'll pick you up at the airport on Tuesday." Then Podres explained that he and Zimmer were planning to take in some races at Saratoga, just a few miles south of Johnny's home. At that famous track his son John drives trotters and pacers. Curt Schilling, the Red Sox pitcher, whom Johnny coached early in his career, owns one of the horses the younger Podres drives. Half a century later, Johnny and Zimmer still play the horses as they did when they were "Boys of Summer." The day after the recent Saratoga outing, Johnny didn't have much to say about his wagers.

"Zim held his own," was all he would offer, but the two of them have a lot of stories about the tracks.

"One time after a day game in Brooklyn, Zim and I drove out to Long Island to bet on the trotters at Roosevelt Raceway. We each had our salaries of about $600 that we got earlier that day.

"At the track we didn't have reserved seats so we watched the races and bet from the bar, and whenever we ordered a drink we always threw back the change for a tip.

"Well, we didn't win a thing and we blew all our dough. When we drove back and got to the toll booth for the Brooklyn Battery Tunnel, I said to Zim, 'You got a dime'?

"Zim says he hasn't got a cent of change, only a $20 bill, and I didn't have a dime—or a $20 bill either. So I told the toll collector, look, we are Johnny Podres and Don Zimmer of the Brooklyn Dodgers and we blew it all at the track and we don't even have a dime.

"The toll guy, disgusted, shook his head and threw a dime in the basket for us. We got through the gates and I just pulled over to the side of the road and had myself a good cry over the whole thing. Now it's pretty funny, but it wasn't then.

"Anyway, I want to tell you about the other guys in '55. Reese was the captain and he will always be the captain of the Dodgers, even though he's gone now. He was a great man. PeeWee was my first roommate. The Dodgers must have thought pretty highly of me to room me with PeeWee, who was 34 in '53. They wanted me to be with somebody who was a good influence." Hanging on the wall in Podres' living room is a signed photograph of PeeWee from that period, inscribed "To my roommate—I think—PeeWee Reese."

"Junior Gilliam and I both came up in '53 and Robby moved to third to make room for him at second. He was a helluva player. He was some leadoff guy. He would really make the pitcher work.

"You know, sometimes I would go out drinking with Junior, and I even fixed him up with a really beautiful girl in Chicago. We had a good time in Chicago because with day games (there were no lights at Wrigley Field then) we always had the night off.

"Junior was a great pool player. We had this poolroom in Dodgertown and Junior would throw $5 on the table and say "Who wants to challenge the devil?" So Alston would. He was a hell of a pool player, too, and he and Gilliam would put on a show.

"Carl Furillo just did his job no matter what. I remember one game in '53 when we were playing the Giants. Leo Durocher was their manager then and they got in a fight and I thought Carl was going to choke him to death. Leo was turning blue. Somebody stepped on Carl's hand and broke it but he kept on playing with it. He missed a few games but played in the Series with the broken hand. He loved to swing at the first pitch and a lot of 'em were homers. The Dodger Sym-Phony Orchestra guys were always bringing him pepperonis and salamis.

"Snider—what an outfielder he was. They used to argue in New York about center fielders—who was the best, Willie Mays, Mickey Mantle or the Duke. I always thought Snider was the best of them at going and getting those drives. If he didn't get a hit his first time up, he could pout a bit though. But if he got a base hit his first time up, especially if he started out oh and two, you would see him pull three or four sticks of gum out of his pocket and cram them in his mouth and you knew then he would have a good day. He could bunt, too, and he could fly. Today the big slugger outfielders don't know how to bunt but Duke could do it all.

"Sandy Amoros didn't speak much English, but he always smiled a lot and he always had that trademark Cuban cigar. Of course, he made 'the catch' in the '55 Series, but like I have said many times, I knew he would. Gilliam never would have got it I suppose, but Amoros was left-handed and reached out and there it was in his glove. The big thing about it though, more than the catch, was how he fired the ball back to Reese, who doubled up Gil McDougald.

"Alston? Walt was the manager in '55 of course, and he never said much, but you always knew what he wanted. He was a big guy, too, and he let all the guys know it. Of course, Dressen brought me up and I always liked him the most. Years later when I was traded to Detroit it was because Charlie was the manager there. I had a choice of three or four clubs I could go to, but I chose Charlie.

Johnny Podres

"Well, we won 98 games in '55, and I won only nine of them that season. But Alston called me his 'money pitcher' and we had a chance to prove it in the Series. I'll tell you, it made me a much better pitcher, playing with those guys. And I don't mean just because they got me the runs and made the plays. It was just that being surrounded by so much talent made you work harder and play harder. There was no other way, if you wanted to stay on the same field with them."

On September 8, the Dodgers clinched the pennant in Milwaukee, 13 ½ games ahead of the runner-up Braves, and the earliest in National League history. They beat their own 1953 record by four days. Owner O'Malley walked around the locker room shaking hands. "I want to beat the Yankees," he said. "We have to beat the Yankees once some time or another and this ought to be the time."

Captain Reese weighed in. He told reporters, "I think most of us want the Yankees to win the American League pennant just so we can play them. I know, as far as I'm concerned, this may be my last World Series as a player. And I want to go out of this game beating the Yankees."

Would this finally be the year? They ached to beat the Yankees. Winning a World Series that did not include the Yankees would be nice, but unsatisfactory. So most Brooklyn fans agreed with Reese and O'Malley that they wanted to face their long-time tormentors. They nevertheless dreaded another demoralizing defeat, an eventuality envisioned by millions all over the country and even overseas.

Johnny Podres' first baseball card,
1952 Parkhurst #76, pictured with the Montreal Royals.

Brooklyn Dodgers "Picture Pak" 5" by 7" souvenir photo.

Podres, Carl Erskine and Sandy Koufax in the Dodgers clubhouse. (Johnny Podres' personal collection).

Rookie pitchers Jim McDonald and Podres shake hands before Game Five of the 1953 World Series. (Photo by Herb Scharfman).

Johnny Podres

On his 23rd birthday, sitting in the Ebbets Field dugout before Game Three of the 1955 World Series. Johnny pitched a complete game, beating the Yankees 8-3. It proved to be a crucial turning point, as the Dodgers dropped the first two games at Yankee Stadium.

With Brooklyn Dodgers legend Arthur (Dazzy) Vance on the steps of Brooklyn's Borough Hall, January 31, 1955. It was "Dazzy Vance Day" in Brooklyn, a celebration of his recent election to the Baseball Hall of Fame.

Bob, John and Robert S. Bennett

"We Showed 'Em." From left to right: Duke Snider, National League President Warren Giles, Walter O'Malley, Podres, and Gil Hodges at the Dodgers 1955 Victory Dinner in the Hotel Bossert. (Photo by Frank Mastro).

Hundreds of fans from Witherbee, New York and surrounding towns honor Johnny Podres' 1955 World Series triumph, as the hero rides along the town's main street. Banner reads: "The Yanks are Dead! Long Live Podres!" (Photo by Gates Barnet).

The winners of the first four Sports Illustrated "Sportsman of the Year" awards gather on January 10, 1958. From left to right: Roger Bannister (1954), Podres (1955), Bobby Morrow (1956) and Stan Musial (1957).

Don Newcombe and Johnny visit "Buzzie" Bavasi (center) on November 16, 1955. Buzzie doesn't want to listen to their requests for salary increases for the 1956 season. Podres would eventually be drafted into the U.S. Navy.

Bob, John and Robert S. Bennett

Most of the Dodgers' pitching staff during Spring Training, 1957. From left to right: Don Drysdale, Sal Maglie, Clem Labine, Carl Erskine, Ed Roebuck, Don Bessent, Ken Lehman, Podres, and Fred Kipp (UPI; International News Photos, Photo by Herb Scharfman).

Johnny Podres

Johnny warming up in the Los Angeles Coliseum. The Dodgers played there during the 1958 through 1961 seasons.

Bob, John and Robert S. Bennett

1961 Johnny Podres "Bell Brand" Baseball Card.

1961 Los Angeles Dodgers "Picture Pak" 5" by 7" souvenir photo.

Chapter Five
"Thanks, Whitey!"

And so, when the country boy from the small mining village stands alone on the mound in Yankee Stadium in the most demanding moment of one of the world's truly epic sports events, and courageously, skillfully pitches his way to a success as complete, melodramatic and extravagant as that ever dreamed by any boy, the American Chapter of the Order of Frustrated Dreamers rises as one man and roars its recognition.
■ Robert Creamer, *Sports Illustrated*, January 2, 1956

Not only had the Dodgers never won a World Series, in 1955 they faced a group of Yankees players who had never lost one. And to younger Yankees fans it seemed the *franchise* had never lost one. When the St. Louis Cardinals beat the Bombers four games out of five in 1942 it broke a string of eight straight victorious Series appearances, beginning in 1927, the era of Babe Ruth and Lou Gehrig. After the '42 defeat, the Yankees turned in seven World Series victories, four of them over the Dodgers. Manager Casey Stengel led the club to five straight world championships, 1949 through 1953. The Dodgers fell in three of those. Overall, National League teams had won only 18 championships; the A.L., 33. And while the Giants had beaten the Indians in 1954, the National League hadn't won two in a row for 20 years.

To further erode the confidence of Dodgers fans that October, the odds makers called it for the Yankees with lopsided figures. Seemingly to confirm their wisdom, the Dodgers dropped the first two games. No team had won the title after losing the first two games in the past 34 years. In

1921, a Babe Ruth-led Yankees team won its first pennant and the first two games of the Series against the Giants, and then bowed. New York sportswriters made the facts painfully clear—and there were lots of them writing, because New York had seven daily newspapers at the time.

The papers delivered plenty of dire prophecies, such as this one from ex-Yankee Joe DiMaggio: "The Dodgers are crazy, mixed-up kids with a deep psychological block. They can't beat the Yankees in the World Series."

So the headlines hung over Brooklyn like a dark cloud. Dodgers fans were headed for the guillotine, the gallows, the firing squad, the electric chair. Only a miracle reprieve would save them. Only a miracle worker could issue one.

"Newcombe and Loes started the first two games at Yankee Stadium and we got beat," Podres remembers all too well. "After the second game Alston told me to be ready tomorrow, that I was opening in Ebbets Field. I felt just great about it. The fact that he was picking me when we had our backs to the wall was a real compliment. It showed the confidence he had in me."

Hardly anybody else shared Alston's view. Podres failed to complete his last 13 starts (in an era when complete games were expected). He finished only nine of 24 starts, and his regular season, hampered by arm trouble until just before the Series, ended with a record of 9-10, hardly a confidence-building performance.

One man, however, told a different story on that September 30, the 23rd birthday of Johnny Podres. He was Dixie Howell, the Dodgers' veteran backup catcher, who warmed up Podres before the game.

"I told Alston," Howell said, "that John hadn't been as fast for a long time and that his curve was better than it's been all season. He was throwing his change-up better, too." The Dodgers themselves remained upbeat.

"Even when we lost the first two games our guys were still confident we were going to win. We figured once we got them in Ebbets Field we'd knock them around a little," Podres recalled. "After the season ended, I had no idea I'd be starting in the Series. We had Newcombe, Erskine, Roger Craig, Loes, and Spooner. I honestly didn't think I'd get a start. I really didn't have an outstanding year in '55. I started off okay, winning seven of my first 10, but then hurt my shoulder. I was on the disabled list for awhile, and when I came back it took me some time to get squared away. For awhile my shoulder was so sore I couldn't sleep.

"Then when I was okay again and getting back into the groove, I got slammed on the foot by a line drive and had a swollen left instep. Then I had a freak accident in September, at Ebbets Field. Batting practice was over and we were getting set to take infield. I had a fungo bat and was going to hit fly balls to the outfielders. Well, in Ebbets Field they used to wheel the batting cage across the diamond and out through a gate in center field. They started wheeling that thing and they hit me right in the side with it. Banged up my ribs pretty good, plus a severe muscle pull. For two or three weeks I could hardly breathe. It was so bad they were thinking of bringing somebody up from Montreal and putting me back on the disabled list, which would have kept me out of the Series. But then after we'd clinched the pennant I pitched a game against the Pirates and had real good stuff so they decided I was okay. Sometimes when I think of how close I came to not playing in the '55 Series I break out in a cold sweat."

For the third game, the sky was gloomy over Ebbets Field, considered a graveyard for lefties, and so was the gathering of 34,200—most of them Brooklyn faithful depressed by losses in the first two games. To make matters worse the wind blew briskly to the left field wall as a left-handed pitcher whose last complete game was back in June took the mound.

All Johnny did was go the route with a seven-hit, 8-3 victory, giving up just two earned runs and striking out six. Half of those whiffs went to leadoff hitter Bob Cerv, who entered the game with a .301 season average. Campanella and Robinson led an 11-hit attack.

"Podres struck me out with every pitch he had," Cerv said after the game. "I know it's no time to grin but I can't help from laughing over the way he did it. Johnny fanned me the first time with a change, the second time with a curve and the third time with a fastball. If he had another pitch and if I had gone to bat another time he probably would have used it and got me."

"I never had a better assortment of stuff," Johnny said when the game was over. "The change-up was my best pitch. I usually throw it only about four or five times during a game but when I found out early that I could get it over I relied on it all afternoon. I guess I showed 'em I could go nine innings. They keep saying I can't go nine. That makes me mad. I didn't feel tired once today."

Campanella put it this way: "Let's say it was the most important victory of Johnny's life, but I've caught him when he was just as good and maybe better. He was good and fast though, this afternoon, and that's what made his change-up so effective."

Reese was extremely high in his praise. "I never saw him pitch so well. It was one of the finest pitching performances I've ever seen anywhere. Speed alone won't beat the Yankees. You have to give them that soft stuff and mix it up and Podres sure mixed 'em up. He had 'em off stride all the time."

In a post-game interview Stengel readily agreed with Reese. "We just got beat because that lefthander mixed 'em real good."

Alston, pleased beyond measure with his first World Series victory, agreed.

"He had good stuff and held it real good. I thought he might be tiring, but when he threw three fast ones past Bob Cerv in the seventh, I changed my mind."

Other Brooklyn pitchers also lauded his performance to the reporters. "I never saw a guy get the change over the way Johnny did today," Russ Meyer said. He's got a terrific motion on this pitch and the fact that he had such good control of it made his fastball and curve much more effective."

Podres was the birthday boy but the present went to Brooklyn.

One Brooklynite summed up newfound confidence the next day in a newspaper letter. "Can you imagine," he wrote, "Johnny Podres goes to bed Thursday night 22 years old and wakes up Friday 23 and beats the Yankees. You couldn't blame him either because as long as a guy has to work on his birthday he might as well spend it in Ebbets Field. Don't believe all those jokes the comedians on television tell about Brooklyn. All those television shows come from New York or Hollywood."

The Dodgers continued to put on a real show in Brooklyn, winning the next two games and taking a 3-2 Series lead back to the Bronx. Snider, Campanella and Hodges led a 14-hit barrage featuring a three-run homer by the Duke for the Dodgers' second Series win. Still in Brooklyn, they took their third Series win with a 5-3 victory featuring another Snider homer. Only one more win in the next two games would give the Brooks their first Series title. Brooklyn fans had heard that one before.

Back in the Stadium, Whitey Ford put the brakes on the Brooklyn express, 5-1, by throwing a four-hitter while the Yankees scored all of their five runs in the first. Skowron hit a three-run homer. Karl Spooner failed in front of 64,022 and the Series was tied.

"Later, when I thought it over," Podres told us recently, "I realized that Ford gave me a chance to be a hero. So for years I have always said, 'Thanks, Whitey.'

"Alston had told me that if we didn't win the sixth game he wanted me to pitch the seventh," Johnny recalled, "so I knew what lay ahead of me. The guys were down after that sixth game, especially Reese. I had to say something, so I told him not to worry I'd shut them out tomorrow. What the hell, you've got to say something at a time like that.

"And I didn't worry about it that night. I never used to think about the next day's game. Why worry today about tomorrow? If I had been a 20-game winner, there would be a lot of pressure on me because I'd be

Johnny Podres

supposed to win. But there was no pressure on me. If I lost they would have said how would you expect him to beat the Yankees twice?"

But his pulse accelerated when he got to the Stadium. And his confidence, never a problem, was bolstered further when Bob Sheppard announced a Yankees lineup without Mickey Mantle. Of course, it didn't help that Robinson was also hurt, putting Don Hoak at third for the decisive game.

"I told Dixie, 'There's no way that lineup can beat me today.' I guess I was trying to give myself a little boost."

Because the Yankees started lefty Tommy Byrne, Alston went with right-handed hitter Zimmer at second and switch-hitter Gilliam in left.

Podres' father and two uncles drove the 275 miles to the Stadium from Witherbee. At her sister's home upstate, his mother and his sister and three brothers and Johnny's girlfriend watched on television from a station in Schenectady that also beamed the game into Vermont.

"When I beat them 8-3 I threw a lot of changeups and I knew they would be looking for it. I threw a few at first and then I went to the fastball and Campy told me to stay with it, especially when the shadows stretched across the field."

At 12:30 it was time for Johnny to warm up. The Dodgers dressing room was deserted except for the pitcher and Campanella, who discussed the hitters.

"Just get that changeup over like the other day," Campanella said. "Get it over and you got nothing to worry about. That'll set 'em up for the other pitches."

"Don't worry," I told him. "I'll get it over. Get me one run and I'll win." Clem Labine recently confirmed that Johnny had made this bold prediction.

Campanella certainly helped get the runs. His first hit of the series, a double, became the Dodgers' first run. His sacrifice moved the second into position.

In the Yankees' half of the second inning, Moose Skowron doubled with two outs but Podres got the next batter. In the third, Podres walked Phil Rizzuto and Billy Martin singled to right. With a 3-1 count to Gil McDougald, Alston walked to the mound.

"'Keep it down,' Alston told me.
"On his fists," I said. "I got my control."

McDougald hit a slow roller to third and the ball hit the sliding Rizzuto for the third out and Podres was out of the inning. Back on the bench Podres told his third baseman, "That was a break, Hoakie."

"'I think I could have thrown him out anyway,' he answered, but it was good that he didn't have to try."

In the Dodgers' sixth, Hodges hit a sacrifice fly that scored Reese, to make it 2-0, and before the inning was over, Alston, looking for power and more runs, sent Shuba in to bat for Zimmer. So when the Yanks came to bat in the sixth, Gilliam moved to second. Amoros, in a fateful move, went into left field.

Billy Martin walked on four straight balls. McDougald dropped a perfect bunt. Berra came to the plate. Reese, Campanella and Alston joined Johnny on the mound.

"Reese asked me if I was all right. I nodded to him. Then Walt asked Campy if I had anything left. Campy told everybody to take it easy. Then he told Walt, 'He'll be all right.'"

"Then Walt told me not to let Berra pull anything—not to give him anything good." Berra, a left-handed batter, was known to pull everything, even outside pitches well off the plate.

"But," Johnny recalled, "the son of a gun lifted a ball out to left field. When he hit it I just bent over and picked up the rosin bag and told myself, 'Well, there's one out.'

"But then I looked around and saw the ball keep slicing toward the line and I saw Amoros running his tail off."

Berra's fly was high and so near the line it looked for a time like it would drop for a foul and that Amoros wouldn't reach it.

"The ball seemed to hang up in the air forever and Amoros is still running. All of a sudden I started getting this sickly feeling that maybe he wasn't going to be there when the ball came down.

"But he was. At the last moment he reached out and that baby dropped right into his glove. I let out a sigh. I guess I had been holding my breath."

The little Cuban stretched out his right, gloved, hand and the ball dropped into it, but the best was yet to come. There is practically no room between the foul line and the low concrete wall topped by the steel fence in the left field corner. He used his free left hand to brace himself against the fence, just in front of the 301-foot mark. Then he rifled the ball to the infield.

"Martin hadn't gone too far off second but McDougald, who was on first, was sure the ball would drop. He was going around second when Amoros caught it. Reese ran out behind third to take the throw.

"Just before he got the ball from Amoros, Pee Wee took a quick look around to see where the runners were. He took a perfect peg from Sandy. I'm still standing there on the mound. All this is happening in a matter of seconds. I'm watching it like everybody else. PeeWee whips around and fires that ball to Hodges at first base. There's McDougald trying to get back. PeeWee made a perfect throw and we had McDougald nailed from here to Christmas. Amoros tried to explain the catch several times in his broken English. But the one I liked best is the way it looked to me. He said, 'I just run like hell.'

"My pal Zimmer to this day takes credit for the whole thing. He says, and can you believe this, that *he* was responsible for the catch and the entire World Series victory! He says that if Alston didn't bat Shuba for him, Gilliam wouldn't have moved to second and Amoros never would have been in left.

"Anyway, boy, did that juice me up. I got the next guy out, got them out in the seventh and eighth, then nailed the first two men in the ninth. One more to go. I was so hopped up I could hardly stand still out there. I just knew I was going to get that last batter and couldn't wait. It was Elston Howard. I wanted to finish up with a strikeout but he kept fouling them off. Campanella called for another fastball but I shook him off. It was the only time in the whole game I did that."

After the game, Campanella said, "That boy had the last word. He sure did."

Podres went into his classic big windup, with his right leg kicking as high as his left elbow. Then he reached back, with the ball as low as his left knee. Howard was looking for high heat, an aspirin. But Podres threw him a bitter pill, his signature pitch, the one that got him there.

A change-up.

Howard hit it down to Reese at short.

"When Pee Wee saw the ball coming at him a big grin broke out on his face. I guess he couldn't help it. He made a low throw to first but Hodges picked it up without any trouble.

"A lot of what happened after that is a blur. I wish I could remember it all, because I'm sure I had a hell of a good time."

What happened after that was captured on film for all time. Johnny leaped straight up in the air from the third base side of the mound, facing Hodges at first, his arms outstretched, his number 45 on his back facing half of the 62,465 fans. Like a star he had become, he hung in the air above the mound for an instant.

When he descended, his catcher reached him before his magnetism drew a crowd.

The renowned sports writer Red Smith, watching from the press box on behalf of *The New York Herald Tribune* and a syndicate that sent his column nationwide, described what millions saw on television:

"All of a sudden he was lost from sight in a howling, leaping, pummeling pack that thumped him and thwacked him and tossed him around; hugged him and mauled him and heaved him about until Rocky Marciano (the undefeated heavyweight boxing champion) in a mezzanine box paled at the violence of this affection.

"Now there was mufti in the swirl of gray flannel as kids materialized from nowhere and adults swept down on the field behind them and it seemed that Podres, caught in the eye of this hurricane, could never be brought through to the sanctuary of the dugout."

Then Smith, America's best sportswriter at the time, reflected:

"One has to pause for a moment and consider before the utter implausibility of this thing can be appreciated. First, the Dodgers never won a World Series and especially they had never won one from the Yankees, not in five meetings over 14 years. Unpredicted to begin with, it became impossible after the Yankees won the first two games. No team in history had ever recovered from such a disaster within the limits of seven games. Then, after the Dodgers accomplished the wildly improbable feat in taking the lead three games to two, the Yankees ground them down again.

"If hope wasn't stone cold dead in the marketplace, faith certainly was."

Myrt Power, a 71-year-old grandmother from Buford, Georgia, who won $32,00 for her baseball knowledge on the popular television program of the day, "The $64,000 Question," wrote in the *New York Journal-American,*

"I been countin' back over the real big days of my life. There's been some big ones all right like when I got married and days like that, but yesterday takes its place with the biggest and I can't think of a thrill that was more thrillin' than the moment my Dodger honeys took the World Championship. How about that little Johnny Podres, who pitched with his arm and head and heart and made history for Brooklyn. My honey Johnny, who is only 23, was as cool and as calm as though he was at a church supper. He just mowed 'em down."

Then there was Joe Williams, who wrote in the next day's *New York World Telegram*:

"At precisely 3:43 in Yankee Stadium yesterday afternoon a king died and an empire crashed, and from Greenpoint to Red Hook, from Sea Gate to Bushwick, from Coney to Flatbush, in fact all over the teeming turbulent borough across the bridge, joy was at once unconfined and unrefined.

"For the first time since the creation of man, a Brooklyn team had become the undisputed ruler of baseball. An interminable frustration that threatened to plunge the citizenry into mass neurosis had mercifully come to an end. At long, agonizing last everything was copasetic in this, the best of all possible worlds.

"In the final analysis, they won because of the stalwart pitching of Johnny Podres, who first saw the light of a change-up in Witherbee, New York. No masterpiece was his performance, but in the clutches he was magnificent, poised, implacable, adroit."

More succinctly, the *New York Mirror* headline proclaimed in big, black type:

**DODGERS
DOOD IT**

And the *Daily News* in even bigger, blacker letters exclaimed on the front page rather than asked:

WHO'S A BUM!

And on the back page, known for headlines just as big as on the front:

THIS IS NEXT YEAR

The New York *Post* ran a full, tabloid-size page photo of Johnny waving to the crowd under the three-inch headline:

PODRES! (Need We Say More?)

Bob, John and Robert S. Bennett

The Box Score of the Seventh Game of the 1955 World Series:

BROOKLYN DODGERS

	AB	R	H	RBI	BB	K	PO	A
Gilliam, lf, 2b	4	0	1	0	1	0	2	0
Reese, ss	4	1	1	0	0	1	2	6
Snider, cf	3	0	0	0	0	2	2	0
Campanella, c	3	1	1	0	0	0	5	0
Furillo, rf	3	0	0	0	1	0	3	0
Hodges, 1b	2	0	1	2	1	1	10	0
Hoak, 3b	3	0	1	0	1	0	1	1
Zimmer, 2b	2	0	0	0	0	1	0	2
a-Shuba	1	0	0	0	0	0	0	0
Amoros, lf	0	0	0	0	1	0	2	1
Podres, p	4	0	0	0	0	0	0	1
Total	29	2	5	2	5	4	27	11

NEW YORK YANKEES

	AB	R	H	RBI	BB	K	PO	A
Rizzuto, ss	3	0	1	0	1	0	1	3
Martin, 2b	3	0	1	0	1	0	1	6
McDougald, 3b	4	0	3	0	0	1	1	1
Berra, c	4	0	1	0	0	0	4	1
Bauer, rf	4	0	0	0	0	1	1	0
Skowron, 1b	4	0	1	0	0	0	11	1
Cerv, cf	4	0	0	0	0	0	5	0
Howard, lf	4	0	1	0	0	0	2	0
Byrne, p	2	0	0	0	0	2	0	2
Grim, p	0	0	0	0	0	0	1	0
b-Mantle	1	0	0	0	0	0	0	0
Turley, p	0	0	0	0	0	0	0	0
Total	33	0	8	0	2	4	27	1

a-grounded out for Zimmer in sixth
b-popped out for Grim in seventh

Brooklyn	0 0 0	1 0 1	0 0 0 - 2	
New York	0 0 0	0 0 0	0 0 0 – 0	

	IP	H	R	ER	BB	SO
Podres, W, 2-0	9	8	0	0	2	4
Byrne, L, 1-1	5 1/3	3	2	1	3	2
Grim	1 2/3	1	0	0	1	1
Turley	2	1	0	0	1	1

Error: Skowron. Double play: Amoros, Reese and Hodges. Left on base: Brooklyn 8, New York 8. 2B: Skowron, Campanella, Berra. SAC: Snider, Campanella. SF: Hodges. WP: Grim. Umpires: Honochick (A), plate; Dascoli (N), first base; Summers (A), second base; Ballanfant (N), third base; Flaherty (A), left field; Donatelli (N), right field. Time of game -- 2:44. Attendance -- 63,465.

Chapter Six
Beatified in Brooklyn

A Toast to the Star

Breathes there a fan with heart so true
Who didn't say when the Series was through,
Those are OUR boys, our lovely "Bums,"
So blare out the trumpets and beat the drums.

Or is there a town with feelings tense,
That ever "enjoyed" such terrible suspense,
Two defeats standing and two to go,
With spirits and hearts being very low.

But lives there a team with determination
That could win the applause of the entire nation
By sweeping three games at Ebbets Field
And by winning the seventh their class was revealed.

Throws there a pitcher with heart so stout
Who could win two games and shut them out,
A toast to the star, Johnny Podres, by name,
The Champ of World Champions of undying fame.

--Alyce Mace, Brooklyn, October 1955

Johnny's Uncle Steven Podres appeared inside the clubhouse.

"Where's dad?" the excited pitcher asked.

"Out in the car in the parking lot. Crying."

Three hundred miles north in Witherbee, Johnny's mother was also in tears. His girlfriend, Naomi Baker, exulted.

A horde of television cameramen, newspaper photographers and reporters waited inside the clubhouse. The players blasted in. More than 200 persons threw their arms in the air. They pushed against the walls. You could scarcely move around. The television crewmen grabbed Johnny Podres and plopped him on a trunk that served as a stage for Frank Frisch's post-game broadcast. The other Dodgers shoved their way to the back of the room, drawn there by cans of cold Rheingold and Schaefer beer. Walter O'Malley and Buzzie Bavasi squeezed their way from one player to another to extend congratulations. Don Newcombe held a can of beer higher than anyone and roared louder than any of the others. Coach Joe Becker jumped on a chair and led a series of cheers.

Podres, cornered in his woven metal locker after the Frisch TV interview was over, kept panting and pleading that "I'm too pooped to say anything," and then they couldn't shut him up. Finding his way through the throng of Dodgers uniforms was a pin-striped Yankee. Yogi Berra hugged and congratulated the Brooklyn pitcher.

"Podres was good all right," Berra said, but he was better last time. We got three runs off him on Friday and were shut out today, but we had him in more trouble this time."

Then he whined, "If only I had got a couple of hits in the sixth and eighth, when we had two men on, we'd have had Johnny out of there. We didn't help ourselves."

If only. Yeah, if only. But, in Berra's defense, it should be pointed out that he was the lone Yankee offering congratulations in the Dodgers dressing room. He wasn't the only Yankee with plaudits, however. Phil Rizzuto, whose 52nd World Series appearance that wonderful day set a record, allowed that Johnny "wasn't better all the way today, but he was terrific when he needed. That kid really showed us something."

Yeah, and he showed it all the way.

Then some of the Yankees began to sound like the Dodgers of years and years before, especially losing pitcher Tommy Byrne: "We'll get those Dodgers next year."

Next year would have to wait. This was Johnny Podres' big moment and he was higher than the proverbial kite. He was exuberant. He was pumped. Cameramen and reporters kept cornering him in the steamy

Johnny Podres

dressing room. But he would squeeze past them now and again and create a scene for a crazy movie that runs too fast.

"Wow!" he whooped and bounced up and down. "Wow. Wow. Wow. I'll never forget this all my life! What a wonderful thing to win the World Series."

Wonderful, indeed. Wondrous, too, because the Yankees were the losers this time. Johnny certainly wowed them on the mound that day, becoming what no other Dodgers pitcher had ever become.

He was the Yankee killer.

"Hey, Pee Wee," he shouted, "what did I tell you? I told you they wouldn't get a thing off me, didn't I?"

Yogi Berra told us recently,

"John was a pretty darn good pitcher. He's the reason the Dodgers finally beat us. He had a real good change-up and good curve and knew what he was doing. He's a good man, all the Dodgers were good guys and we respected them. I went into their clubhouse after they beat us, congratulated Pee Wee and Jackie and they were almost in tears. I think they always felt that year was their last chance to beat us. They were aging a bit. I remember telling John he did a tremendous job, because he did.

"Of course, my ball that (Sandy) Amoros caught in the left-field corner was the biggest play. I'd heard later that (Walter) Alston would've taken John out if Amoros hadn't made that catch. The Dodgers were playing me to pull and I went the other way with an outside pitch. Never thought Amoros would catch it - only reason he did was because he was their fastest guy and was left-handed. Don Zimmer always likes to say he's the real reason the Dodgers won, because if he wasn't taken out for a pinch-hitter, Jim Gilliam would've still been in left and he wouldn't have caught my ball. Instead Gilliam moved to second to replace Zim. Amoros was put in left in the sixth just before we got up. Well, John stayed in the game and finished the job pretty good."

Roger Craig remembers Reese in tears, along with Robinson, Snider and Hodges, "because it took so long to beat the Yankees."

Then the reporters trapped Johnny again with questions.

"Yes, my fastball was my best pitch in the late innings. No, I wasn't nervous. How could I be when the skipper told me he wanted me to pitch the seventh game and stood by me the way he did? This was one I had to win."

Then he bounced around the room some more.

"Wow, wow, wow. Hey Duke, are you going to stay out all night like me? Let's have ourselves a time.

"Wow! What a catch Sandy made. Wow.

"Hey Bulb-Eyes," he called to third base coach Billy Herman. You sure waved them in today. Wow!

"Phew, I'm tired," he allowed. Then he slumped down on the bench as reporters fired more questions.

Then he got even more excited as the significance of the event began to penetrate the dressing room steam.

"My dad was here today. He was nervous this morning. I told him not to worry and I waved to him in the stands a couple of times to let him know we had them.

"You know, my dad was a really great pitcher. He could have pitched in the big leagues if he ever had a chance. He had a great curve, as good as Erskine's."

Just then Joe Podres walked in, along with his brother Steve and another of Johnny's uncles, Anthony Glebus. Joe, a hard-working iron-miner, was 45 then and some thought he looked more like Johnny's brother than his dad.

"Dad," Johnny shouted, "how did you like that?"

Then they "wowed" together and the father and son hugged and cried. Always devoted to his dad, Johnny proved that day he had listened when his father spoke and watched when his father pitched.

Other Dodgers pitchers were in awe of the scene. Roebuck remembered it in detail although he candidly said 50 years later what winning the World Series really meant was he earned a $9,700 share, which was significant compared to his $6,500 annual salary.

Russ Meyer told the happy lefty's father:

"Mr. Podres, you must be the proudest man in America. That kid of yours has more guts than the law allows."

"I always dreamed something like this would happen," the senior Podres said. "I always wanted Johnny to be a champ—and he is."

Johnny beamed, looked at his dad and said, "You were a little nervous out there, though, weren't you, Pop?" And to the assemblage, "He was so jumpy I was afraid he'd leap out of the stands or something."

"You're a hero now!" a teammate yelled at him. "You're the talk of the country. They'll all be after you for TV appearances."

"Okay," the excited pitcher hollered, adding with a newly crowned hero's 23-year-old bravado, "for a thousand dollars a throw.

"Now I'm really popping off." There was no stopping him.

"My fastball really had it. Mantle? I wasn't worried about him. I keep my fastball up on him and he can't hit it. I was never really worried about anybody. I can beat these guys seven days a week.

Johnny Podres

"I never once doubted I could take 'em. Sure, I was in a tight spot once in a while. But all I had to do was bear down."

The bouncing Podres was so high his feet barely touched the floor. A few years later when Cassius Clay leaped wildly over a prone Sonny Liston in Lewiston, Maine, those witnesses that day in the Dodgers dressing room and millions of television boxing fans saw a similar scene. At this moment, Podres was the greatest. His performance was a similar knockout of a big ugly team by an improbable kid opponent.

Finally, he ventured outside to board the team bus from the Bronx back to Brooklyn.

"I was in the middle of all these cops outside," he recalled, "and I said 'Look at this. This is something else'.

"I remember getting on the bus and everyone giving me a hand, the players and their wives. It was touching, really touching. It was some day in Brooklyn Dodger history."

And it was some celebration in Brooklyn that night.

Announcer Vin Scully, a Fordham grad and at home in the Bronx, was quoted in "Bums No More," Stewart Wolpin, St. Martin's Press, 1995:

"When the Yankees won a World Series, the Bronx didn't go bananas, and when the Giants won in their great hey day, I don't think Manhattan danced in the streets. But when Brooklyn won the World Series, the borough went wild. It was like us against the world.

"After the last game in Yankee Stadium we were driving back toward Brooklyn. And you could almost see the lights coming on in Manhattan. Football was just around the corner and everything was very quiet.

"But suddenly when we went through the Brooklyn Battery Tunnel and came out on the other side it was a whole, new, world. Dancing in the streets. It was like VJ Day (just 10 years earlier). I mean, the joy in the streets, the block parties, the streets roped off.

"We had to park, as I remember it, about two blocks from the (Bossert) hotel and we had to walk. The police had set up sawhorses and everything else. There were hundreds and hundreds of people on the sidewalks and they were cheering and screaming. It was an incredible night."

Inside the Bossert, hotel personnel were readying a victory party for the players, wives and team personnel. Outside, 2,000 cheering fans pressed against police barricades. Meanwhile, the number of phone calls (Did you hear? Did you see *that*? Remember that bet? You owe me.) exceeded in volume, if not in excitement, those of VJ Day.

Those not calling family or friends ignited firecrackers and banged spoons on frying pans, just as little kids did when World War II ended. It seemed everyone not in the streets stood on doorsteps (or "stoops," as they called them). Some turned pillows into Yankee effigies and strung them up from lampposts. Office workers tore up telephone books and threw the pages out of the windows. Tickertape became fluttering confetti.

Free hotdogs and kegs of beer appeared on the streets while horns blared and motorcades proceeded up and down major thoroughfares. Factory whistles and church bells joined the cacophony and then traffic came to a complete stop as a seven-block gridlock lasted an hour and a half.

While hundreds, then thousands danced in the streets, poolrooms and bars filled up with revelers filling up on beer and every other type of booze. Women danced on the bars. Cigar smoke pervaded the air, much of it from free stogies handed out at several stores. Rodney Dangerfield was nowhere to be found.

Borough citizens tossed their heads back and then held them high. It was the peak moment in Brooklyn history. Fifty years later it has yet to be matched. Perfect strangers in a metropolis known for wary residents eyed each other and broke into huge, delighted grins. Grown men wept openly. Everybody was simply shocked. They were just numb.

The 23-year old kid who was the chief architect of all this jubilant chaos says he remembers little about the celebration that night, but Brooklynites of the day would never forget it.

Clem Labine recalled,

"The celebration was mammoth. There were tons of cars and people on top of cars."

Before he went to the Bossert party the irrepressible young lefty appeared on the "Tonight Show," whose Manhattan host was Steve Allen. Then he joined the grand dinner dance inside the hotel and kicked up his heels, dancing with the daughter of Dodger executive Fresco Thompson.

Joan Hodges, Gil's widow, recalled special moments of the evening for us and said, "John was the nicest boy you would ever want to meet." Told about that 50 years later, Podres laughed.

"Nicest *boy*? What was she, 28 or something?"

But Joan remembered that fans outside the hotel clamored for a glimpse of their heroes and that Gil and Johnny made sporadic appearances out front, waving to thousands and signing autographs.

"Somebody," she said, "cut Johnny's necktie off all the way to the knot. And when they went outside everybody just went crazy."

Outside, Johnny said, "There was one old guy who told me over and over he had been waiting for this since 1918.

"It was a helluva party. The champagne was really flowing."

Johnny Podres

Johnny had always known how to have a good time, and now he had all of Brooklyn, the whole country and pockets of baseball geography elsewhere in the world willing to help him. In the days and weeks and years to follow he endorsed fishing tackle, cigars and other products ("Most of which I never even used," he told us), downed endless free meals and drinks and addressed a variety of civic groups. Only the speechmaking was troublesome.

"I could pitch to Mickey Mantle before thousands at Yankee Stadium and millions on television—no problem. But I got nervous making a speech to a couple of hundred." His first opportunity to fidget at a microphone came in his hometown.

On Saturday, October 8, rainclouds threatened Mineville, up in the Adirondacks, and the day was raw. None of the 4,000 Johnny Podres' friends and neighbors and townspeople and fans noticed the weather; they focused their attention on their hometown boy. It was Johnny Podres Day at Linney Athletic Field (now known as Johnny Podres Field). The crowd converged on the site of Johnny's boyhood baseball exploits from throughout Essex County, New York. Witherbee, Johnny's home, population 1,500, sent a big contingent. Mineville, population 800, and Port Henry, with 2,000 citizens, were well represented. They couldn't take their eyes off the stalwart son of Anna and Joseph Podres, residents of the area all their lives and the proudest parents anywhere.

The celebration began at noon with a parade from Johnny's home to the field. He and his parents rode in an open convertible through the winding streets of the company towns where just about everybody worked for Republic Steel.

The politicians, including representatives to the State Assembly in Albany, took advantage of the situation, of course. William Dwyer, principal of Massena High School, who was principal at Moriah High and helped Johnny get into pro ball, was another speaker.

Johnny made a speech of about 150 words. He thanked everybody for everything and said he was sorry he couldn't make a better speech because that was the one thing his old high school coach, Steve Kazlo, the former Fordham backfield star, had failed to teach him.

"Today is the proudest day of my life. Maybe some day, some way I can show you what this day has meant to me."

Twice during the celebration, first as he got into the car and again after the parade got going and confetti fell on the car, he couldn't hold back the tears. Neither could his parents.

What was really in his heart?

"I was worried whether the kids I grew up with would think I had changed into some kind of big shot, a big city guy. That was the farthest thing from my mind. I always wanted to live up here where I can see the clouds on the mountain tops, where I can fish through the ice in the winter, where I can hunt deer and rabbits.

"Sure, I wanted to make money out of baseball, but I always wanted to be right here where I had more friends than I can find anywhere in the world."

Immediately following the fabulous victory, admirers and opportunists flooded the young pitcher with telegrams. Here are just a few.

"YEA. WITHERBEE MINEVILLE CONGRATULATIONS. GREATEST VICTORY EVER. PRAYING FOR YOU ALL THE WAY. PROF. DWYER."

"TRIED TO CONTACT YOU TODAY BY PHONE. FIND IT IMPOSSIBLE. IMPORTANT YOU CALL ME IMMEDIATELY REGARDING LUCRATIVE TELEVISION AND THEATRE ENGAGEMENTS. EXPEDIENCE ESSENTIAL. CONGRATULATIONS. WILLIAM MORRIS AGENCY INC. LEE SALOMON."

"PLEASE CALL ME VIA OPERATOR 267 IN CHICAGO. BELIEVE I HAVE A PERSONAL APPEARANCE PROPOSITION OF GREAT INTEREST TO YOU. JOE STERN. HARSHE-ROTMAN PUBLICITY."

"WILL GUARANTEE FIVE HUNDRED DOLLARS TO SHOW IN EXHIBITION GAME SUNDAY OCTOBER 16 IF POSSIBLE. CAN ARRANGE HUNTING TRIP IN MAINE FOR YOU AND YOUR DAD FREE WHERE MANY MAJOR LEAGUERS HUNT. CALL ME REVERSE CHARGES AT PRESS HERALD SP219 SATURDAY OR SUNDAY THIS WEEK. TJ HALES."

"I WANT TO JOIN WITH YOUR FRIENDS AND NEIGHBORS IN WISHING YOU WELL TODAY. YOUR PITCHING WAS GREAT. ALL NEW YORKERS PROUD OF YOU. AVERILL HARRIMAN."

The honors quickly followed. Johnny was selected Most Valuable Player of the World Series. Even today, half a century later, you can spot his New York license plate on the back of his Cadillac sedan. It says "MVP 55."

There was, of course, the '55 Corvette that went to the MVP. He gave it to his father, who traded it in for a sedan.

The biggest prize was announced on the cover of Sports Illustrated, along with his photo. Johnny Podres beat all comers in every field of athletic endeavor to become *Sportsman of the Year* for 1955.

He was the second to receive the award. Roger Bannister won the first one for cracking the four-minute mile barrier. Subsequent winners over the past 50 years have included Muhammed Ali, Arnold Palmer, Michael Jordan, Sandy Koufax and Orel Hershiser (the only other Dodgers—pitchers, mind you—to gain this accolade).

In fact, over the 50 years since the inception of the award, only 14 other baseball players won it until 2004. That year they gave the honor to the entire Boston Red Sox team, which turned in a post-season that probably has come the closest in history to approaching the drama that occurred in 1955. Podres applauded the selection. "It was a great team effort," he told us the day after the announcement.

The following season would not be one to bask in the warmth of adulation around the National League, however. Podres was not to be found on any major league mound. The Dodgers would somehow win the pennant without him, but not the World Series. Johnny was conspicuous by his absence for sure. When it really counted, Dodgers pitching would come up short against the Yankees once more.

Chapter Seven
From Swabby to Shut-out and ERA King

Early in 1956 Johnny joined the Navy in what may have been the result of a sinister campaign. The military draft was in effect. Some people wrote letters to newspapers wondering how a World Series MVP could have a back so bad he couldn't serve in the armed forces. Others decried the draft board reclassification from 4F to 1A, including Ted Williams, the Red Sox star who had been a Marine fighter pilot hero in both World War II and the Korean War. Ted was disgusted, called the decision "gutless," and told Johnny he was conscripted only to remove him from the Dodgers' mound.

It was good news for the rest of the National League, and, as it turned out, for the Yankees when October arrived. No question about it, Podres was missed during the '56 World Series as much as he was needed in '55.

Sent to Bainbridge, Maryland, Johnny soon wound up in a Navy hospital because the rigors of boot camp aggravated his bad back.

"First they put me in the hospital, and then they told me to go to the beach and relax. I spent most of the time in civilian clothes."

As he began to feel better, he donned uniforms again—a baseball uniform for the Bainbridge Naval Training Station, and another for the Norfolk Naval Base team. That summer he served his country by serving up fastballs, curves and changeups. He won 14 games against Navy teams and lost one—and that was a beaut.

Bob, John and Robert S. Bennett

"I struck out 25 batters in 12 innings, and we lost 1-0 to a pretty good lefthander, but I can't remember his name."

It's a pretty good bet the lefty remembered John.

The Navy gave Johnny an honorable discharge under medical conditions in late October when it was too late to kill the Yankees in the World Series again.

"That winter I told Bavasi I weighed over 190 and hadn't thrown a baseball since I got out of the service. Of course, it was as cold as 20-below up in Witherbee, but I was working out every day in a gym.

"At Vero Beach in February of '57, I was soon throwing easily and freely and getting the ball over the plate. By March, I was really back in the groove. I threw three innings against the Tigers in relief of Newk and gave up only an infield single. I also knocked in a run and we won easily."

"During the month they matched me up as a starter against the Yankees' Don Larsen, who pitched the perfect game in the '56 Series."

A record Vero Beach crowd turned out for the exhibition.

"I didn't give 'em a hit for six innings. Then Drysdale took over and continued the hitless pitching."

Larsen had allowed four hits through five innings and was relieved by Tommy Byrne, who matched up against Podres in the '55 Series seventh game. Byrne gave up two more hits but the Yankees didn't have any until there were two out in the ninth.

Then none other than Byrne lined a single through the right side. Drysdale also gave up a single to Tony Kubek in the 10th inning of this scoreless affair, and Don Bessent took over in the 11th, putting the Yanks down in order.

In the bottom of the 11th Don Demeter doubled and scored the game's only run on an error to the delight of the Florida Dodgers fans.

Podres' six-inning stint was the longest of the Dodgers pitchers that spring. It ran his string of scoreless innings against the Yankees to 17, going back to the '55 Series, showing he could kill the Yankees in the pre-season as well as the post-season.

Before the month was over Johnny pitched a one-hit shutout against the Redlegs for seven innings, but Erskine relieved and gave up two runs in the eighth for a Cincinnati win. Johnny hadn't given up a hit for 12 innings until Gus Bell singled in the seventh.

Before spring training was over Johnny pitched five strong innings against the Braves and four more against New York as the Dodgers beat the Yankees again.

Johnny Podres

The '57 regular season was about to begin, and it would be one of the best for the lefty. It would also be his last in Brooklyn. On April 20 he struck out nine Pirates and gained his first victory, a 2-0 complete game. It was his first appearance before his Ebbets Field fans since he became the '55 Series hero. His fastball and his change of pace did the job. The Pirates got only six scattered safeties and two bases on balls. Only one Pirate got as far as third. It was the first complete regular season game for a Dodgers lefthander since Koufax turned one in on September 3, 1955.

A couple of futile starts followed. On May 3, he gave up only five hits to the Cards in six innings, but the Redbirds broke through because of a Dodgers error. Johnny left for a pinch hitter in the seventh. The game went 12 innings before St. Louis won it, 3-2.

His second complete game shutout came at the Polo Grounds in the middle of May, bringing his record to 2-2. The Giants managed only six hits, two by Willie Mays, and the Dodgers won, 5-0. On the 21st, he registered a complete game 6-1 win over Cincinnati. He went to only one full count and walked nobody, the first time he had done that. On the 26th Willie Mays doubled, tripled and homered and the Giants won, 8-7, but on the 29th he notched his third shutout of the young season, the most in the National League. It was a three-hitter, all singles, over the Pirates.

Another three-hit shutout followed, 4-0 over the Phils, and now he had more shutouts than any other pitcher in the majors. It was the second time in the month he ended a four-game losing streak with a shutout. Again, the hits were all singles and nobody reached third base. He struck out nine. The record was 5-2. Watching, in the Philadelphia grandstand, was Jackie Robinson. He retired the year before, in rejection of a trade to the hated Giants. The decision was extremely pleasing to Dodgers fans. The very idea of Jackie in a Giants uniform was repulsive.

A June 9 victory over the Redlegs, 9-2, put the Dodgers in first place. Johnny's scoreless string after two straight shutouts ended at 22 innings in the fourth and Frank Robinson homered in the eighth. But there was no denying his sixth win (five in a row) against the two losses. Meanwhile, his earned run average was a measly 2.03. Six singles rattled around the Ebbets infield and outfield in a four-run fourth on June 17 and Podres' pitching arm and the Dodgers fell to the Cardinals in the second game of a doubleheader.

"Three days later the team doctor told me I had a deep tendon pull in my left elbow that would require heat treatments and rest," he remembered. His 6-3 record was the best on the club but it was not known how long he would be off the mound.

"About three weeks later I started relieving, to get me back in action a little at a time," he recalled. "In my first game back I went in and gave up a double but struck out the next guy with three fastballs. You don't forget times like that because you wondered how you would make out."

On the 12th he pitched the last two innings of a 5-4 victory over Cincinnati in Brooklyn. He allowed one hit in the eighth, then got the next four batters to pop up, after Danny McDevitt, Clem Labine, Roger Craig and Newcombe took turns on the mound. Today he would be credited with a save for that performance.

On July 15th he was still relieving. He took over for Sal Maglie in the ninth in a tie game. When Gil Hodges homered in the bottom of the ninth, Johnny got his first career win over the Braves, a 3-2 affair.

Ready to start again, five weeks after his last one, Johnny threw a five-hit, 1-0 shutout in St. Louis on July 23rd. The fifth shutout gave him the major league lead in that department once more. It was his eighth win and his first complete game in St. Louis in eight career starts. The Dodgers swarmed around Podres after he retired Stan Musial, Del Ennis and Ken Boyer in order in the bottom of the ninth.

Johnny went the route again five days later for a 7-2 victory over the Redlegs in Cincinnati at Crosley Field. Carl Furillo smacked a grand slam in the Dodgers' eighth and Ted Kluszewski nicked Johnny for a solo shot in the bottom half of that inning. It was Johnny's sixth complete game triumph on the road. He had allowed only three runs in 43 away-game innings and lost only one game away from Ebbets Field. Podres allowed nine hits but Frank Robinson and Johnny Temple each had three.

On the first of August Johnny threw a six-hitter at the Braves in Milwaukee and allowed only one run, unearned, but Gene Conley fired a four-hit, 1-0 shutout. Conley, the 6' 10" sometime Boston Celtic, singled in the only run after a throwing error by Reese put a man on base. Podres' record stood at 9-4.

A week later at Ebbets Field, the Dodgers failed for the second time in a row to score a run for Podres. The major league shutout leader (five) was on the losing end now.

"I got the first two batters in the sixth inning of a scoreless tie with the Giants," Johnny recalled. "Then I walked Hank Sauer. Bobby Thomson lifted a long drive. It looked catchable until the last second, and Sauer wouldn't have been running if there hadn't been two outs. But it went for a triple and Sauer scored."

Even though Johnny had given up only three hits and already had one of the Dodgers' five hits, Alston pinch-hit Amoros for him in the seventh.

Sandy popped up. The Giants got four hits off Labine in the final two frames.

It was loss number five for Podres, but both teams, who had announced they were heading west the next season, were losing fans. The weather was ideal, but only 18,000 witnessed the contest between the New York City archenemies.

Johnny had a 3-0 lead in the sixth inning against the Pirates a week later, but his late-season back problems emerged and he gave up a single and a double for a run. Alston summoned Labine, who gave up a sacrifice fly, then a homer in the ninth to tie the game. The Pirates won it in the 10th.

The Dodgers, who played some games in Jersey City in 1956 and '57, won there on the 16th when Johnny beat the Braves 4-1. He gave up only five hits through the eighth but a walk and a single in the ninth, bringing Roebuck to the mound.

"Those were the days," Johnny recalled, "when relief pitchers actually provided relief. Nobody was counting pitches then."

Eddie retired the last two batters for what today would be a save. It was Johnny's 10th victory against five losses. Only 8,500 watched.

Johnny's next three starts left him with two losses, at the hands of the Braves and the Giants, but on September 6th at the Polo Grounds he returned to form. Johnny gave up only three singles in a full-route shutout, his sixth of the season, tops in the majors. He didn't allow a hit after the fifth, struck out four and walked two. It was "only" his ninth complete game of the season. His record was 11-7.

On September 11 Ernie Banks smacked his 37th homer for Chicago, depriving Johnny of his seventh shutout, but he beat them 9-1. Only two other Cubs got as far as second base with the five-hitter for his 12th win. Meanwhile, Johnny collected three hits, including a double (the Brooks' only extra-base hit), and knocked in a run. It was his first win of the year against the Cubs and now he had beaten every team in the league during the season. The run was the only one he allowed in the last 18 innings.

A week later in Cincinnati, Johnny left a 2-2 game in the 10th. Roebuck walked in the winning run. Johnny had allowed seven hits, but singled and doubled on his own behalf and the record now stood at 12-8.

Roebuck did it again on the 22nd. Johnny pitched into the ninth, giving up only two runs, but Roebuck walked in the winning run again. Johnny knocked in Don Zimmer with a double in the fourth, but the rest of the Dodgers left 10 men on base and Johnny with a 12-9 record.

Rookie Rene Valdes started for the Dodgers on the 28th, but couldn't get through the fifth inning against the Phils. Roebuck relieved him. In the ninth, with the Dodgers ahead, 8-3, Roebuck walked in a run and left with the bases loaded and two outs. In came Podres in something of a role reversal with Roebuck. But Podres was Podres and he whiffed the final Phillie, preserving a victory for Roebuck.

The '57 Dodgers finished in third, with a 84-70 record, 11 games behind Milwaukee. Snider (40, 92, .274), Hodges (27, 98, .299) and Furillo (12, 66, .306) continued to hit, but Reese and Campanella continued to decline. Charlie Neal and Gino Cimoli cracked the lineup as regulars. Besides Podres, only Drysdale (17-9, 2.69) and Roebuck (8-2, 2.72) pitched brilliantly. Newcombe won 11 games and lost 12, and no other pitcher won more than seven games.

So ended the final Brooklyn season. Los Angeles would get a team that won six pennants in ten years, finished second three times and third twice (including '57). They would also get a pitcher who won the team's only World Series, taking a 1957 record of 12-9, a league-leading earned run average of 2.66 and a major league leading half a dozen shutouts to the West Coast. In 196 innings of 31 games, Johnny allowed just 64 runs. He also was in the league's top ten in strikeouts per nine innings. Brooklyn fans, who got another excellent performance from their biggest Dodgers hero, bade Johnny a fond farewell. Owner Walter O'Malley? That was another story. In Brooklyn over four decades later they still hated O'Malley. But they still loved Johnny Podres.

Chapter Eight
Way Out West

After the 1957 season, the Dodgers' move to Los Angeles broke the hearts of the Brooklyn fans. Brooklynites still recoil at the mere mention of Walter O'Malley. You'd have thought he had kidnapped their only child with no chance for ransom. In fact, the borough that had forfeited some of its identity when it became part of New York City now had lost most of the rest of it. Even to this day, in the minds of many, Brooklyn had lost its soul.

While O'Malley offered to build a new, privately financed stadium, Brooklyn land values increased exponentially since Ebbets Field opened in 1913. O'Malley asked the City of New York to condemn the land near Atlantic and Flatbush Avenues, under the authority of Title I of the Federal Housing Act, to drastically reduce costs. One of the most powerful bureaucrats of the 1950s, Robert Moses, rejected O'Malley's demands, which interfered with his own plans. Moses was hell-bent on the Dodgers moving to Flushing Meadows, Queens, site of the 1939 World's Fair.

"O'Malley wanted a new stadium at Atlantic and Flatbush, but the City wouldn't approve it," former Brooklyn and Los Angeles Dodger catcher Joe Pignatano recalled.

"Now they're building basketball courts there. Moses said O'Malley was bluffing because he had a 'goldmine' in Brooklyn. The politicians took O'Malley's 'bluff,' and the people of Brooklyn blamed O'Malley, instead of the politicians."

The idea of the "Queens Dodgers" rang hollow, and throughout the 1956 and 1957 seasons, O'Malley solidified alternate plans to build his dream stadium in Los Angeles. O'Malley also persuaded Giants president Horace Stoneham to relocate to San Francisco, finally opening the West Coast to major league baseball.

On October 7, 1957, it was official, as the Los Angeles City Council approved a deal for the Dodgers to build a new stadium in Chavez Ravine.

Many of the Dodgers, including Pignatano and Podres' roommate, Clem Labine, lived in Brooklyn with their families and were not happy to leave. Podres also hoped the Dodgers would remain in Brooklyn, closer to his home in Witherbee. During his Brooklyn years, Johnny often made the five-hour drive from New York City to Witherbee, usually stopping at Massie's Restaurant in Glens Falls for spaghetti and meatballs. Once the New York Mets began playing in 1962 (first at the Polo Grounds and then, lo and behold, in Flushing, Queens), he made the same trip whenever possible.

In the off-season, Johnny always retreated to Witherbee, and could usually be found at the town firehouse, playing basketball and pinochle, or enjoying a drink at the bar. Podres did enjoy Los Angeles, especially the nightlife and the Santa Anita and Hollywood Park racetracks. Johnny was a devout bachelor at the time, and Witherbee lacked the fancy watering holes and glamorous women that appealed to many major league baseball stars. As Dodger teammate Wally Moon stated,

"Off the field, John was hard to keep up with." Joe Pignatano recalled,

"Johnny was happy-go-lucky and liked to drink. And Don Zimmer and Johnny were always off playing the ponies."

"Everyone blamed me for being a wild man because I was single, but most of the other guys were partying too," Johnny countered.

Upon arrival in Los Angeles, Podres and Labine rented an apartment, hosting a few good parties, sometimes with Gil Hodges as bartender.

"John was a bachelor and behaved like one," Labine said recently. "I missed my children. Although I liked the City of Los Angeles, I would much rather have stayed in Brooklyn."

Even in Los Angeles, the players usually did not hobnob with celebrities. But, as Podres recalls,

"Many stars (including Nat 'King' Cole and the 'Rat Pack' of Sammy Davis Jr., Dean Martin, and Frank Sinatra) attended Dodger games as a status symbol."

Only Chuck Connors, television's "Rifleman," who played in one game for the Brooklyn Dodgers in 1949, would visit the clubhouse. Podres remembers Connors as having "probably the foulest mouth" he ever heard. Johnny also recalls a young Clint Eastwood's developing interest in Dodger baseball and near-regular attendance at home games.

The era of the Los Angeles Dodgers began with tragedy. On January 28, 1958, catcher Roy Campanella was paralyzed for life when his car slid off an icy highway and into a light pole, near his home in Glen Cove, Long Island. Campanella was a three-time National League Most Valuable Player (elected to the Hall of Fame in 1969), and his injury (coupled with the retirement of Jackie Robinson after the 1956 season), marked the informal ending of the Brooklyn Dodgers era.

"Campy was an excellent catcher, both offensively and defensively. He always made things easier for his pitchers and called a great game. Roy would set up exactly where the pitch should be thrown. And he always knew how to help his pitchers in tough situations," Johnny recalled.

John Roseboro, who appeared in 35 games for the Dodgers in 1957, would succeed Campanella as the starting catcher. Campanella lived until 1993, and Roseboro passed away in 2002.

Back-up catcher Rube Walker recalled the transition from Brooklyn to Los Angeles:

"The team might have been changing all along, but I didn't really notice it until we got to Los Angeles."

Don Drysdale, Sandy Koufax, and rookie Stan Williams joined Podres in the rotation.

"Just five years before it was Podres who was our young pitcher and now he was the veteran," said Walker.

Pignatano, who went on to coach the New York Mets for many years before retiring in Brooklyn, also recalls working with Podres and the Dodgers' younger pitchers.

"Johnny was always around the plate and his ball was as light as a feather. You could catch his pitches with tweezers or a kleenex, he was very easy to work with."

Clem Labine noticed Podres' continuing development as a moundsman:

"He had good control, and a good idea of what he was doing, including when to pitch inside or out. He knew his hitters. When his curve was sharp, you knew he would be having a good day."

In 1958, the Dodgers held spring training at Holman Stadium in Vero Beach, as they had done every year beginning in 1948. On March 5, Podres, Snider and Zimmer were injured in an automobile accident (the third in three months involving Dodger players, including Campanella, and a February crash in California involving rookie Jim Gentile and his family).

The three suffered minor injuries as they tried to beat a 12:30 a.m. curfew. Podres twisted his neck and required seven stitches to close a gash on his forehead. The crash resulted when Snider drove a Swedish sports sedan, in a poorly lit section of town, over a railroad track. A train that left Vero Beach Station was 500 yards away, but came to a halt in plenty of time for Snider to back the car off the tracks.

During the construction of Dodger Stadium, the team would play at the Los Angeles Memorial Coliseum, a track and field stadium built for the 1932 Olympics. The odd-shaped baseball diamond had a left field fence of only 251 feet, although a 42-foot high screen was installed, making it a more difficult target. Center field was 425 feet away, with right center at 440, crushing left-handed power hitters, such as Duke Snider. The Coliseum was tough on most left-handed pitchers as well, but Johnny Podres grew to love it.

"Lots of balls that hit the screen would have been home runs in most other ballparks," Johnny said.

He became the most successful left-hander in the short history of the Coliseum, winning 29 games. Most of the other Dodgers pitchers detested pitching there, including Labine.

"It did not matter if you were a right or left-handed pitcher," Clem said, "the Coliseum forced you to pitch differently. For example, you couldn't go inside and had to pitch outside most of the time."

On April 16, 1958, at Seals Stadium in San Francisco, formerly a Pacific Coast League park, Podres delivered the Los Angeles Dodgers' first victory, a sweet beating of the hated Giants, 13-1, on homers by Snider and third-baseman Dick Gray. Two days later, the Dodgers debuted at the Coliseum before 78,672 fans, beating the Giants again, 6-5. Gray had hit the first Los Angeles Dodgers home run:

"It was a 3-0 pitch and I nailed it," Gray recalled.

Gray also remembered Podres as "probably one of the better pitchers that the Dodgers ever had" and that Podres possessed "the best change-up of any pitcher."

On June 3rd, Los Angeles city voters passed a referendum, "Proposition B," which ratified the city's original October 7, 1957 agreement. The referendum permitted O'Malley to proceed with his plans to build Dodger Stadium in Chavez Ravine. The rest of the 1958 season brought few highlights. With most of the players making a difficult adjustment to the West Coast, 1,845,556 fans passed through the turnstiles. The Dodgers finished 71-83, seventh in the eight-team National League, scoring only 668 runs while allowing 761. Only a late-season collapse by the hapless Phillies saved the Dodgers from their first last-place finish since 1905.

Winning 10 games at the Coliseum, Podres led the team in earned-run average (3.72), wins (13, the ninth most in the National League, against 15 losses), and strikeouts (143, tied for the league's third best). Fourth in the league in strikeouts per nine innings with 6.12, John was named to the All-Star team for the first time. Roseboro, who hit .271 with 14 homers, was the only other Dodger selected. Unfortunately, neither got a chance to play, and the American League won 4-3, at Baltimore's Memorial Stadium.

Overall, Dodger pitching was mediocre in 1958, with a 4.47 team earned-run average. Don Drysdale and Sandy Koufax won 12 and 11 games, respectively. Drysdale also helped the offense with seven homers, slugging .591. Newcomers included 22 year-old Larry Sherry and 21 year-old fireballer Stan Williams. In the bullpen, Labine went 6-6 with 14 saves.

A couple of other Brooklyn stalwarts didn't fare too well. Roger Craig was limited to nine games, and Don Newcombe was 0-6 with a 7.86 ERA before being shipped to the Reds on June 15th. In exchange for "Newk," the Dodgers received Johnny Klippstein, Steve Bilko, Art Fowler and Charlie Rabe. Bilko excelled in the Pacific Coast League, and the Dodgers hoped he would provide some power. While he hit seven home runs in 47 games, Steve batted only .208 and in 1959 was selected by the Detroit Tigers in the Rule V draft.

A victim of the long right field porch, the after-effects of knee surgery, and recurring knee problems, Duke Snider was limited to 106 games, batting .312 and slugging .505, but with only 15 homers (in each of the five previous seasons, he hit at least 40). Gil Hodges smacked 22 homers (tying second baseman Charlie Neal for the team lead) and Carl Furillo hit .290 with 18 dingers, but wore himself down running around the gigantic Coliseum outfield. PeeWee Reese played his last 59 games before retiring at age 40, while Ron Fairly, 19, and Frank Howard, 21, played their first major league games.

After the season, the Dodgers acquired Wally Moon from the Cardinals for Cimoli. Moon was a left-handed hitter who adapted his stance so that he could launch "Moon-shots" over the left field screen. The dimensions of the Coliseum were altered for 1959, with right-center brought in from 423 to 375 and the right field foul pole changed from 390 to 333 feet.

On December 23, the Dodgers traded minor league second baseman George (Sparky) Anderson to the Philadelphia Phillies for Rip Repulski, Jim Golden, and Gene Snyder. The 1959 Phillies became one of the legendary "worst" teams in history, while the Dodgers catapulted to first place.

L.A.'s First Pennant

The '59 Dodgers became Walter Alston's all-time favorite squad and the source of his proudest managerial achievement. At the home opener on April 14, the Dodgers set a night-game attendance record when 61,552 fans watched Cardinals pitcher Lindy McDaniel beat Podres with a six-hitter, 6–2. But the Dodgers ended up with a record of 11-6 during the month of April.

On May 7, 1959, the Dodgers and the New York Yankees played an exhibition game for "Roy Campanella Night." Before a record crowd of 93,103, money was raised for Roy's medical bills and rehabilitation. Reese guided Campanella's wheelchair into the ballpark and "Campy" addressed the crowd:

"I thank God that I'm living to be here. I thank every one of you from the bottom of my heart."

After he spoke, the lights went out and nearly every fan lit a match in his honor.

The Dodgers struggled in late May, rebounded in June (as a seven-game winning streak brought them within a game of first place), but fell back to third place by the All-Star break.

On August 24, Koufax struck out 13 Phillies in the first of three record-setting outings. While (according to Johnny Podres), Nat "King" Cole danced on the Dodger dugout, Sandy fanned 18 Giants on August 28, tying a single-game record. He then proceeded to whiff 10 Cubs on September 6, for a total of 41.

In late September, the Dodgers swept a three-game series with the Giants, ending the Giants' pennant hopes (always a satisfying achievement!). In the final game of the series with San Francisco, on September 20, Johnny Podres notched a key victory, defeating "Sad" Sam Jones (a 20 game winner) 8-2, with relief help from Koufax and Sherry. The win propelled the Dodgers into first place for the first time since July, but it was short-lived. Traveling to St. Louis, the Dodgers dropped the first game of the series, yielding first place to Milwaukee. Then, on September 26, the Cubs put the pennant race into a tie by blasting the Dodgers 12-2 at Wrigley Field, racking up 18 hits against Podres. In the last game of the season, Roger Craig beat the Cubs 7-1, setting up a three-game playoff with the Braves, as Milwaukee beat the last-place Phillies 5-2.

The playoff series began in Milwaukee on Monday, September 28th. In the first game, Roseboro's home run in the sixth inning put the Dodgers ahead for good 3-2. Sherry got the win with seven and two-thirds scoreless innings in relief of Danny McDevitt.

At the Coliseum for the second game, Drysdale faced Lew Burdette, who was especially tough on Dodger hitters. Needing a victory to stay alive, the Braves led 5-2 after eight innings. In the bottom of the ninth, Moon, Snider and Hodges each singled, knocking out Burdette, and Norm Larker blasted a two-run double off the left field screen against reliever Don McMahon. Manager Fred Haney brought in Warren Spahn, hoping for a save, but Alston countered, sending up Furillo to pinch hit for Roseboro. Alston's move paid off, as Carl hit a sacrifice fly to tie the game.

In the bottom of the 12th inning against Bob Rush, Gil Hodges walked with two out, and Joe Pignatano stepped to the plate. Pignatano stated,

"The first pitch was up in my eyes, but the next pitch was letter high and I hit it up the middle for a single. I always liked the ball upstairs."

Furillo then hit a bouncer up the middle that Felix Mantilla gloved, but bounced his throw past first-baseman Frank Torre. According to Pignatano,

"Mantilla made a helluva play, but his off-balance throw hit Torre on the arm." Hodges scored and Vin Scully shouted into the microphone,

"We go to Chicago!"

The Dodgers finished the season with a record of 88-68, scoring 705 runs and allowing 670. The team also led the league in attendance with 2,071,045. Trading for Moon proved a key element in the Dodgers' success. He hit .302 with 11 triples (sharing the league lead with teammate Charlie Neal), 19 home runs, and 74 runs batted in, finishing third in the league with a .394 on-base percentage.

Hodges led the team with 25 homers (winning a Gold Glove award at first base) and Snider hit 23, slugged .535, and batted .308. Second baseman Neal won a Gold Glove award, smacked 19 HRs, and hit .287. In his first full season, Don Demeter blasted 18 homers. Gilliam led the league in walks and batted .282 with 23 stolen bases. Brooklyn stalwart Furillo was limited to 90 at bats, but still hit .290, and Larker contributed in a reserve role, batting .289 with eight homers. Maury Wills was called up to replace the slumping Don Zimmer (who hit only .165 through 97 games) and hit .389 during September.

Johnny Podres remained the ace of the pitching staff, racking up 14 wins against nine losses (the eighth best winning percentage in the league), with a 4.11 earned-run average and 6.69 strikeouts per nine innings, third best in the National League. He struck out 145 batters, for seventh best in the N.L.

Roger Craig experienced his finest season with an 11-5 record in 17 starts, and a stellar 2.06 ERA, which would have been the league's best had he pitched enough innings. Drysdale, the workhorse, threw 270 innings, going 17-13, with a 3.46 ERA, and four shutouts (tied for the league lead). His 242 strikeouts led the majors. Koufax, 8-6, with a 4.05 earned-run average and 173 strikeouts (third best in the league) and McDevitt (10-8, 3.97 ERA) rounded out the starting staff. Twenty-two year-old Stan Williams also made 15 starts, compiling a 5-5 record and a 3.97 ERA.

The bullpen, however, was problematic. Labine went 5-10, with only nine saves. Fowler, Klippstein, Snyder and Chuck Churn each allowed five runs or more every nine innings. Sherry was 6-7 at St. Paul, Minnesota (one of the Dodgers' minor league teams) when Alston called him up to the majors. After getting beaten in his first two starts, he didn't lose another game, and Alston decided to use him in the bullpen as the "stopper." In 14 games, he was 5-0 with three saves and a 0.74 earned run average over 36 1/3 innings. In a late-season appearance in relief of Podres, he pitched eight and two-thirds innings of shutout ball, knocked in three runs with a home run and two singles, and defeated the Cardinals 4-3.

With only one day to celebrate and travel to Chicago, the Dodgers were exhausted. Still, Podres and Zimmer made sure to place a few bets at the track. As Churn recalls,

"After a short workout, Johnny, Don Zimmer and myself decided to go to the racetrack. They bought a program and began to study it. I barely knew how to read one. I picked four out of the five races and caught hell for not giving them the tips. It was all luck on my part!"

Now retired and living in Virginia, Churn remembered,

"Johnny was one hell of a pitcher, and was at his best when the chips were on the line. He had a change-up that rates among the best, is a great friend, and was one heck of a roommate!"

The 1959 American League Champion "Go-Go Sox" were managed by Hall of Fame member Al Lopez, who played for the Brooklyn Dodgers from 1928 to 1935. The White Sox won 94 games, relying on pitching, speed, and defense. They finished five games ahead of the Cleveland Indians and fifteen games ahead of the Yankees, for their first pennant since the "Black Sox" scandal of 1919. The team stole 113 bases, but lacked punch, with only one regular (Sherm Lollar) slugging over .400. Nellie Fox hit .306 to lead the offense, Luis Aparicio stole 56 bases, and Lollar cracked 22 home runs (the only other player in double-digits was Al Smith with 17).

On the pitching side, 39-year-old Early Wynn was 22-10 with a 3.17 ERA, Bob Shaw went 18-6 with a 2.69 ERA, and Billy Pierce won 14 games. Turk Lown and Gerry Staley anchored the bullpen, combining for 29 saves. The Sox featured an interesting array of support players, from veterans Ted Kluszewski, Larry Doby, Del Ennis and Ray Boone, to youngsters Norm Cash, Earl Battey, J.C. Martin, and Johnny Callison.

Bye-Bye Sox

The 1959 World Series opened in Comiskey Park on October 1, 1959, before 48,013 fans. Craig started the game for the Dodgers, which ended in disaster, 11-0. Kluszewski smashed two home runs and sparked a seven-run third inning. The Dodgers committed three errors and were completely shut down by Wynn and Staley (who relieved in the eighth). Many believed that the Dodgers were overmatched, and would easily be defeated.

In the bus ride back to the hotel, Zimmer quipped,

"Go-Go Sox, my ass!"

But according to Labine, who pitched a scoreless inning in the loss,

"The team was still confident after Game One. We liked getting away from the Coliseum, but having 92,000 fans helped a lot when we did play there."

And Johnny Podres was ready for action in Game Two. It was October 2, with 47,368 fans in attendance. Shaw, the Sox' second-best pitcher, took the mound for Chicago and promptly retired the Dodgers in the top of the first inning.

In the bottom of the first against Podres, Aparicio doubled. Nellie Fox then flied to Larker, with Aparicio moving to third. After walking Jim Landis, Podres could have been out of the inning, but a double-play ball by Kluszewski hit Neal in the chest and he fumbled it. The only play was to first base, and Aparicio scored. Then, Lollar singled just past Neal, scoring Landis. It looked like another White Sox rout was on the way.

In the top of the second, with two out and Wills on base, Podres hit a bloop single to center field just over Fox's glove. Unfortunately, Kluszewski made a somersault catch on Gilliam's foul smash to end the inning. Over the first four innings, Shaw stymied the Dodgers on a few singles.

Podres settled down after the first, allowing only three hits over the next five innings, including a single to Bubba Phillips in the sixth that tailed down the left field line, fair by inches. In the fifth, Neal redeemed himself, hitting a memorable home run into the left field stands. Trying to catch the ball, a fan accidentally spilled a cup of beer over outfielder Al Smith's head. White Sox 2, Dodgers 1.

In the top of the seventh, with two out, Alston decided to pinch-hit for Podres, even though Johnny had pitched six strong innings. Former

Stanford linebacker Chuck Essegian, who hit only one home run in 85 at-bats during the season, was sent to the plate. Alston said,

"We were a run behind, there were two out, and it was getting late. I wanted somebody who could hit the ball out of the park."

The 5'11" 200-pound Essegian promptly did so, tying the game. Essegian recalled:

"The pitch was up and I hit it into the upper deck in left center. Podres and Shaw both pitched a great game. I don't think I had ever faced Shaw before, and the truth is, I just got lucky. And it's a thrill for me to remember that I was pinch hitting for Podres, a great pitcher and a great guy."

Today, Chuck Essegian is semi-retired as a lawyer, still doing some legal work.

"I still follow baseball, but not as closely as I used to. The thing I miss most about baseball is being around all the great guys, like Podres, that I met."

Unsettled, Shaw walked Gilliam, and Neal stepped to the plate. Charlie sent a blast over Landis' head in deep center field, over the 415-foot sign and into the White Sox bullpen, as the Dodgers moved ahead, 4-2. Shaw (today a developer of commercial real estate in Palm Beach County, Florida) stated recently that Neal was the toughest Dodger batter he faced during the Series.

But the Sox weren't finished. With Sherry on the mound in the bottom of the eighth, Kluszewski singled to center and Lollar followed with a single off Gilliam's glove. Lopez sent Earl Torgeson in to run for Kluszewski. With the count three-and-two, Al Smith whacked a double between Moon and Snider that hit the left field wall on a bounce. Torgeson scored. Moon threw a perfect strike to Wills and Wills whipped the ball to Roseboro, waiting to tag the slow-footed Lollar. Third-base coach Tony Cuccinello, another former Brooklyn Dodger player, admitted it was a mistake to wave Lollar home, stating,

I thought it would take a perfect play to beat him."

The play was almost perfect, although Lollar might not have scored even on a somewhat sloppy play. Sherry struck out Billy Goodman, and retired Landis on a foul pop to Roseboro, to end the inning.

"With the score 4-3, Smith on base, and one out, I was able to pitch out of it," recalled Sherry. In the ninth, Sherry retired the side in order, preserving the victory for Johnny Podres. As Sherry remembered,

"I had no trouble in the ninth. It was the turning point of the series, some say, and I got the save for Podres."

Chuck Essegian recalled,

"Johnny Podres was a great pitcher and never got the credit he earned and deserved, probably because the Dodgers had such a great pitching staff. I remember that we had lost the first game by a big margin and we needed to win that second game. As usual, John came through with a great game, like the champ he is. On a personal level, Podres is a great guy and I'm really fortunate to have been his teammate. I have very fond memories of Johnny."

Wally Moon reflected,

"Johnny was an excellent left-handed pitcher and my personal feeling was: If I need one particular win, I would like to give the ball to 'Point!'"

Don Demeter, now the pastor of a Baptist church in Oklahoma City, recalled that,

"Johnny was the guy you gave the ball to for a must-win game. He was great to play behind, because he worked fast, with no fooling around on the mound. He knew how to pitch, how to set up a hitter, and had the best change-up I ever saw."

Norm Larker, who is still in contact with a few old teammates and "occasionally" attends a Dodger game with his family, said,

"John was one of the most competitive pitchers that I played with. If I had to pick one guy to pitch in a big game it would be him."

The first World Series game on the West Coast was played at the Coliseum on October 4, before 92,394 fans. Drysdale faced Dick Donovan, an excellent pitcher with a 3.66 ERA during the season, despite a 9-10 record. Through the first six innings, Donovan faced the minimum 18 batters, while Drysdale countered with seven scoreless innings.

In the bottom of the seventh, Neal singled to left and Larker and Hodges walked to load the bases. Staley relieved Donovan and Alston sent in Furillo to bat for Demeter. Furillo rifled a base hit up the middle, scoring two runs.

In the eighth, Sherry relieved Drysdale and ended a Chicago rally that resulted in a run. The Dodgers scored again in the bottom of the inning, and Sherry struck out the side in the ninth, leading the Dodgers to a 3-1 victory. The White Sox scored only one run on 12 hits, and left 17 men on base.

In Game Four, Wynn and Craig faced off in a rematch of the first game, before 92,650 fans. In the bottom of the third, the Dodgers scored four runs on two-out singles by Moon, Larker, Hodges, Demeter, and Roseboro. Chicago tied the game in the seventh on a three-run homer by Lollar over the left field screen. Leading off in the bottom of the eighth, Hodges slugged his fifth career World Series home run and the Dodgers (behind Sherry, who relieved Craig in the same inning) held on to win 5-4, taking a 3-1 Series advantage.

The largest crowd ever to attend a World Series game (92,706) gathered on October 6, witnessing an incredible pitching duel between Koufax and Shaw. In the fourth inning, Fox scored the White Sox' only run on a double-play grounder by Lollar. In the eighth, the Dodgers threatened. Essegian walked, and Snider grounded into a fielder's choice. Alston sent in Podres as a pinch runner for Snider, and he reached second on Gilliam's single off the left field screen. Johnny believes that he made a base-running error by "getting faked out by Al Smith in left, and holding at second when I should have tried for third."

Podres eventually reached third on a wild pitch, but Shaw was out of the inning after Landis caught a deep fly to right center by Neal, in a spectacular, over-the-shoulder fashion. The White Sox stayed alive 1-0, but the Dodgers kept their Series lead. Pignatano caught one inning of Game Five.

"In 1959, Sandy Koufax was not that wild, just a little high or a little low," Pignatano said recently.

"His curve ball you needed to be on your toes and ready to block, but he threw a very light ball. At that time, he just needed a little more experience under his belt."

In contrast, according to Pignatano, Drysdale threw a very heavy ball, a "shot put."

"Drysdale threw so hard, we knew he wouldn't last long as a pitcher," Joe remembered. (Drysdale retired at age 32 in 1969, was elected to the Hall of Fame in 1984, and died of a heart attack in 1993 while a Dodgers broadcaster).

Clem Labine recalled Campanella's opinions on Koufax:

"We will have a great left-handed pitcher here when he learns to hit me instead of the backstop."

Like Johnny Podres, Labine believes Koufax was the greatest pitcher he ever saw.

"He had the greatest stuff that there was," said Labine.

The Series headed back to Comiskey Park for Game Six, with Podres starting for the Dodgers against Wynn. In the top of the third inning, Snider belted his 11th Series homer, a 400-foot, two-run shot to left, setting a National League record. In the fourth, the Dodgers scored six more runs, beginning with singles by Larker and Wills. It was 4-0 when Podres smashed a long double to center field that hit the warning track and rolled to the fence, scoring Wills from first base. Jim Landis was playing Podres shallow, but the ball was walloped.

Johnny Podres

Donovan entered the game in relief of Wynn, immediately yielding a walk to Gilliam and a two-run double to Neal. Moon followed with a two-run homer to deep right center, and all of a sudden, it was 8-0. Wally recalled that this was a "pivotal moment" in the dugout, instilling confidence that the world championship would soon belong to the Dodgers. Today, Wally is retired and living in Texas, watches an occasional baseball game, and keeps his eye on the standings.

"I'm not a great spectator, I'd rather be doing, so I play golf, fish, hunt and spend time with my family," Moon said.

Wynn brushed back a few Dodgers, and teammates urged Podres to retaliate. In the bottom of the fourth, Podres threw a high and inside pitch to Landis, who moved in on the ball, attempting to bunt. Landis was struck in the head and fell to the ground.

"When he went down, I started shaking" Podres said. "You never want to hit anybody like that."

Landis knew it was an accident, recalling,

"I was worried because I had no idea where I was."

Luckily, Landis was not hurt, and as he pointed to his head, thankful for wearing a helmet, the crowd booed Podres.

"At the time of the game," Landis remembered, "it was a meaningless thing. I talked to Podres later in life, when we were teammates on the 1967 Detroit Tigers, and all that was meant was to brush me back."

Jim Landis is currently retired, lives in Napa Valley, California, and enjoys traveling, playing golf, "and the grandkids."

After the incident, Johnny lost his composure and yielded a two-run upper deck blast to Big Klu that scored Landis and Lollar. After walking the next batter, Podres was lifted by Alston. As usual, Alston asked for Sherry.

"When I was told to warm-up in the fourth, it surprised me," said Sherry.

"I didn't think I would be used that early. Coach Charlie Dressen and Alston figured I was the 'hot hand,' so with the score 8-3, they brought me in from the bullpen in center field. I had a cocky walk, so I was booed all the way in! John was dejected but didn't say anything more than, I think, 'go get 'em' or something like that. I was throwing well and had some gas in the tank, with a big lead. Roseboro called mostly fastballs. I never had a real tough inning the rest of the way."

Sherry allowed just four hits over the last five and two-thirds innings, notching the victory and bringing the first World Series flag to Los Angeles. In the ninth, Essegian pinch-hit another home run to set a World Series record, making the final score 9-3.

"Duke Snider was slated to hit and was up around the batter's box," recalled Essegian.

"Billy Pierce, a left-hander, came in to relieve for the White Sox, and after he came in, Alston told me to hit for Snider. On the way to the plate, I passed Snider, who was coming back to the dugout, and Duke said,

'Nobody has ever hit for me in a World Series game, so you better hit another one!'

"Before Pierce finished warming up, he hurt his arm, and Ray Moore, a right-hander, came into pitch. If I remember correctly, I hit the first pitch he threw, and the ball barely got into the stands in left field. Talk about luck. And just imagine, how many guys can say they pinch hit a home run for a Hall of Famer in a World Series game?"

Sherry relieved in all four Dodger wins, won two games, and compiled a 0.71 ERA in 12 2/3 innings. He was named World Series MVP. Johnny Podres was 1-0, pitching nine and one-third innings, and giving up five earned runs. He batted .500, with a double and one RBI.

In his autobiography, *A Year at a Time*, Alston summed up the 1959 champs:

"They may not have had as much talent as others, but they had tremendous desire. They played like a championship team all the way. They were a manager's dream."

In 1989, in Vero Beach, Florida, the living members of the 1959 Dodgers were invited to meet another "over-achieving" team that became unlikely World Series winners, the '88 Dodgers.

"While playing a round of golf on the first day," Don Demeter told us, "I had a good score, far under what I normally shot, and Johnny made bets that I would beat another player the next day. Johnny didn't realize I had shot way below my usual score. The next day, I shot my normal game and lost. And Johnny lost his bets."

The Dodgers declined in 1960, finishing 82-72, fourth in the National League and 13 games behind the Pittsburgh Pirates. Paid a salary of $22,000, Johnny had a fine season, with a 14-12 record and a 3.08 earned-run average (eighth best in the league). He had 159 strikeouts, and 6.29 strikeouts per nine innings, both eighth best in the N.L. It was the fourth straight season that Podres defeated every team in the league at least once. He also pitched two scoreless innings in the second All-Star game, July 13, 1960, at Yankee Stadium. Podres retired Mantle and struck out Berra, as Alston's National League team won 6-0.

The 1960 Dodgers pitching staff had the lowest earned-run average and the most strikeouts in the majors. Drysdale went 15-14 with a 2.84 ERA and 246 strikeouts, Williams was 14-10 with a 3.00 ERA, 175 strikeouts, and Koufax compiled an 8-13 record, 3.91 ERA, and 197 strikeouts. Craig finished at 8-3 with a 3.27 ERA.

In the bullpen, Sherry won 14 games and saved seven, and Roebuck had eight victories, eight saves, and a 2.78 ERA. On June 15, the Dodgers traded Labine to Detroit for Ray (Baby) Semproch and cash. Before he ever pitched for the Dodgers, the Washington Senators picked Semproch in the Rule V Draft.

For the offense, Larker hit .323, second in the league. Howard hit 23 homers, and Moon hit .299 with 13 four-baggers. Young Dodgers players continued their ascent. Wills hit .295 and stole 50 bases. Twenty-one year old Tommy Davis showed promise with a .426 slugging percentage, and Willie Davis hit .318 in 22 games. Brooklyn-era Dodgers continued to decline: Hodges hit only .198 with eight homers, Snider batted .243 (but still led the team in slugging percentage), and Furillo played his last eight games before being released on May 17th. The "Reading Rifle" later owned a delicatessen in Queens, and worked on the construction of the World Trade Center, before his death in 1989. Another Brooklyn Dodgers hero, Sandy Amoros, was traded to Detroit for Gail Harris, after seeing only limited duty. Amoros retired at the end of the season (and passed away in 1992, at age 62).

Chapter Nine
Victories and Tragedy

To start the 1961 season, Johnny was given a $3,000 raise. His salary was now equal to Drysdale's, and behind only those of Snider, Hodges, and Moon. He was still considered the dean of the Dodgers' pitching staff. Early in 1961, however, Johnny continued to experience back problems, specifically spondyloysis, which he believed resulted from his activities as a pole vaulter in high school.

Columnist Bob Hunter of the *Los Angeles Herald Examiner* referred to Podres as having a "million dollar arm and a ten-cent back." Hunter's column quoted General Manager Buzzie Bavasi:

"Podres is the only pitcher in the world who develops a chronic back ailment every January 8th. He calls me long distance (collect) from Witherbee and moans:

'My back's killing me, Buzz. Send me transportation money so I can get some treatments from Doc Kerlan?' Kerlan must treat him at Santa Anita. That's where they spend the afternoons together."

According to Podres, this story is the opposite of the truth.

"Bavasi called me and asked that I come out to Los Angeles for x-rays on my back," Podres said. "When I got out there, he asked me,

'Are you going to the track today?' I told him yes, and he immediately asked Lee Scott, the traveling secretary,

'Make out a check to John for $500,' giving me some extra spending money for the racetrack. What a great guy, I thought. But then, as I prepared to leave, Bavasi said,

'Hey, wait a minute, before you go you need to sign your contract.' He wanted me to sign a blank contract, so that he could fill in the amount later."

That was a typical negotiating ploy by the crafty Bavasi, one of the great general managers of all-time. Podres had a good relationship with Buzzie, and they remain friends. Podres recalled that Alston once found him out after curfew, with another player, at a "strip joint." Alston sent the other player back to the hotel, and confronted Podres.

"What are you doing here, Walt?" Podres asked innocently. Alston fined him $250.

"But later, Buzzie gave me $500 back," Podres said.

As spring training began, Johnny was peripherally involved in one of Alston's most famous off-the-field incidents. Alston fined Larry Sherry (Podres' roommate at the time) and Koufax (who roomed with Williams) for breaking curfew. Alston checked the room and found Podres, but no Sherry. Johnny called out in a loud voice,

"I'm here, Walt!," which might have been an unusual occurrence, in and of itself. When Sherry returned at 1:45 a.m., he slipped back into the room. Alston was waiting for him, and Sherry slammed the door in Walt's face. Enraged, Alston pounded on the door, breaking his diamond-studded 1959 World Series ring. Alston held a closed door meeting the next day, stating he was "too lenient" with the players. Sherry reportedly was fined $200, and Koufax, $100. Although the press reported that the two were "out getting pizza," Johnny confirms that they were "out on the town" instead.

Despite his back problems, John looked very good in spring training, and coach Joe Becker predicted that Podres would win 20 games.

"I've never seen Podres look better in the spring," Becker stated. Coach Leo Durocher told Podres that he would win "a minimum of 22 games."

In his last spring start, Vada Pinson hit a line drive off Johnny's left wrist. Although x-rays were negative, the wrist was swollen and Podres was in danger of missing his first start of the regular season, scheduled for the second game against the Phillies. But he made the start anyway, striking out 11 Phillies in eight innings and winning 3-2, assisted by Wally Moon's two-run homer. Johnny also collected two hits and drove in the winning run. In his next start, Podres beat the Reds 1-0, pitching eight and one-third innings and smashing a double. Willie Davis made a stunning catch to rob opposing pitcher Joey Jay of an extra base hit, and Moon was the offensive hero with an RBI single. Sherry relieved in both games.

Johnny Podres

Despite suffering a strained left shoulder muscle during his fourth start against Pittsburgh, Podres pitched six shutout innings in a 10-0 blow-out. In his fifth start, against the Phils, he pitched a complete game shutout, winning 6-0. Fairly smacked a three-run homer and added an RBI triple in support.

Podres became the first pitcher to reach five victories without a loss, giving up only eight earned runs in 47 1/3 innings, for a sparkling 1.53 earned-run average. On the return flight from Philadelphia, as the Dodgers jet made its approach over Hollywood Park and gradually descended toward the airport, Durocher quipped,

"Hey Podres, are you going straight to the track, or home to shave first?"

After Podres' five consecutive victories, columnist Melvin Durslag wrote in the *Los Angeles Herald Examiner*:

"You ask the Dodger manager what suddenly has inspired Johnny Podres to pretend he's Warren Spahn, and the manager will shrug and tell you frankly there is no reason in particular.

'Johnny has developed a new pitch, a change-up on his curve', says Walter Alston, 'but otherwise he's the same Podres, simply going in good form.'"

At the time, Johnny told the papers:

"I haven't changed anything but the speeds on my curve and fastball. I take a little off one time and a little more the next, then maybe I'll zing it in. The more I play this game, the more I'm convinced that timing is the key to hitting. And the best way to ruin their timing is to show them four or five different speeds on every pitch you have."

Unfortunately, in his next start against the Braves on May 15, Podres left the game in the fourth inning with a stiff and sore shoulder. It was his first loss of the year, a 7-5 Milwaukee victory. The loss also snapped his scoreless streak of 18 innings. John was forced to miss his next few starts, because an inflamed tendon on the front part of his left shoulder was slow to respond to treatment. His rehabilitation consisted of massages by trainer Wayne Anderson, and cortisone shots administered by team physician, Dr. Robert Kerlan.

On Saturdays during the season, Johnny served as an instructor for Durocher's California Baseball School, at Mormon Temple Field in West Los Angeles. Durocher, Podres and several other Dodgers also appeared on the *Dinah Shore* television show (in a yodeling act), along with actor James Garner. Leo made a habit of guest-starring on television, appearing in the '60s sitcoms *Mister Ed*, *The Munsters*, and *The Beverly Hillbillies*. Koufax and Drysdale also made notable appearances in episodes of *Dennis the Menace* and *Leave It to Beaver*, respectively. For his part, Johnny was not too interested in acting. *Los Angeles Times* sportswriter Jim Murray described Podres as "concerned with the basics of life—an inside straight, a hot horse in the eighth, a rare steak, a new girl on the block."

On June 6, Johnny made his first appearance since May 15, pitching three and one-third innings in relief of Roger Craig. Although he gave up two earned runs, he retired seven consecutive batters and picked up the victory as the Dodgers beat the Pirates, 8-7. With the team in first place, on June 10, Johnny made his first start since the injury. Although the Dodgers beat the Phillies 5-4, Johnny did not get the victory and yielded three earned runs in five innings before Dick Farrell (acquired in May for Demeter and Charley Smith) and Sherry took over.

Podres had no decisions in his next couple of outings, as his sore shoulder did not fully respond to treatment. Dodger physician Dr. Bob Woods stated that Podres was not hurt, but that his shoulder muscles were "rusty."

By late June, Podres claimed that his shoulder problems were behind him and that he was ready to resume his winning ways. John promptly notched his seventh win against the Cubs, pitching five and two-thirds innings and giving up two earned runs in a 4-2 victory. He improved to 8-1 in a 5-2 victory over the Phillies on July 1st, giving up two earned runs in seven and two-thirds innings, and moving the Dodgers to within a game and one-half of first place.

Podres lost his next start to the Cardinals, but advanced to 9-2 on July 8, with a 10-1 complete game victory over the league-leading Reds, striking out seven, and ending the Reds' eight-game winning streak. The only run given up by Johnny was Frank Robinson's fourth inning homer. At the time, Johnny was asked if he thought he would win 20 games.

"A man with back trouble never predicts the future," Podres told reporters. "I don't hear President Kennedy making any predictions on Berlin."

On July 19, Johnny beat the Reds again, 8-3, improving his record to 11-2 and bringing the Dodgers within two and one-half games of Cincinnati. He won his 12th game against the Cardinals on July 23, but was ejected in the seventh inning. According to the *Los Angeles Times*, Podres threw a curveball to Stan Musial that the pitcher believed was strike three, but which was called a ball. After Musial hit his next pitch for a run-scoring single, Johnny "came toward the plate and proffered [Umpire] Pelekoudas a tart vocal Valentine that led the offended arbiter to thumb Johnny out of the game."

Victory number 13 followed on July 28 against Pittsburgh as the Dodgers won 6-4, behind back-to-back home run shots by Snider and Willie Davis. But he dropped to 13-3 against the Giants, as Juan Marichal (assisted by two home runs from Felipe Alou) fired a one-hitter, snapping the Dodgers' eight-game winning streak, 6-0, on August 2nd. The Dodgers moved into first place on August 6 when Podres defeated the Cubs, 11-4, going the distance and picking up his 14th victory. Six days later, Podres grabbed his 15th, pitching a five-hitter and beating the Cardinals 5-1, behind Howard and Moon, who each knocked in two runs. On August 16, the Dodgers blew a double-header to Cincinnati, with Podres losing the nightcap 8-0, the victim of two homers by Gene Freese and one by Darrell Johnson. The Reds' victory placed them a game ahead of the Dodgers in first place.

The Dodgers lost their eighth straight game on August 22, in St. Louis, with Farrell getting tagged with the loss in relief of Podres. When the Dodgers beat the Reds 10-6 four days later, Johnny collected his 16th victory (against four losses), and the Dodgers moved to within one and one-half games of first. On August 30, Johnny beat the Cubs 5-2, bringing his record to 17-4, with Sherry fanning seven of the nine batters he faced in relief. Johnny's record in road games was now 11-0.

Podres' 18th victory came against the Giants on September 3rd, 5-4. It also was his 100th career victory, and he became the winningest Dodgers pitcher since Don Newcombe in 1956. The win put the Dodgers just two and one-half games behind the Reds. The *Los Angeles Times* reported that Johnny had six more starts left, with a very good chance to win 20 games. But on September 8, he lost to the Giants 7-3, bringing his record to 18-5. John gave up homers to Willie Mays and Orlando Cepeda in the first inning and was sent to the showers. He did not receive a decision on September 12, an 11-inning victory over Philadelphia, 6-5.

On September 16, one day before he was scheduled to pitch against the Braves, John was called home because his father was hospitalized with double pneumonia, silicosis, and lung cancer, which probably resulted from working in the mines in upstate New York. Johnny took a red eye flight from Los Angeles to Boston and an uncle drove him to Burlington, Vermont, to his father's bedside at Mary Fletcher Hospital. His father went home from the hospital and John stayed with him for a week, missing two starts. Meanwhile, the Dodgers were almost out of the pennant race, as the Reds' magic number stood at four.

Johnny rejoined the Dodgers to start against St. Louis. Behind 2-1 in the fourth inning, Alston sent Tim Harkness up to pinch hit, which infuriated Johnny. Podres tore into Alston,

"My father is dying and I want to be with him. But I came back to help the ball club, and you take me out of the game!"

Although the Dodgers won 8-5, staying in the pennant chase, Podres advised Alston that he would no longer pitch for him, and that he would leave the club to be with his father. Johnny flew to his father's bedside, but his father died before he arrived. Joseph Podres was only 52 years old.

After his father's death, Bavasi called and pleaded with John to come back, but Podres told him that he would no longer pitch for Alston. Johnny finally did go back, but the season was over. His absence was as significant as his presence in the minds of fans who recalled his 1956 stint in the Navy and that year's World Series loss to the Yankees. The Dodgers finished the season in second place, four games behind Cincinnati, with a respectable 89-65 record. Without Podres' early season injuries and the tragic death of his father, Johnny might have won 20 games, and the Dodgers the 1961 pennant. Podres was the Dodgers' most reliable starter in 1961. He achieved a career-high in victories (fourth in the N.L.) and led the league in winning percentage (.783). He racked up 124 strikeouts, with 6.11 per nine innings (ninth best in the league).

The Dodgers again led the majors in strikeouts, by a wide margin. Koufax enjoyed a breakout season, winning 18 games against 13 losses, with a 3.52 ERA, striking out 269 batters for a National League record. Drysdale's record was 13-10, with a 3.69 ERA, and 182 strikeouts. Right-hander Williams went 15-12, 3.90 ERA, and struck out 205.

Sherry accumulated 15 saves, and Farrell saved ten (but with a 5.06 ERA). Rookie Ron Perranoski was 7-5, 2.65 ERA, and Craig was relegated to the bullpen where he allowed 6.15 runs per game, making him expendable.

For the offense, Moon led the league in on-base percentage at .434, which was matched by 22-year-old Fairly in 111 games. Ron had a breakout season, hitting .322 with 10 home runs. Although Roseboro led the team with only 18 homers, seven other players hit at least 10 (Neal, Moon, Tommy and Willie Davis, Howard, Fairly, and Snider). Wills led the league in stolen bases with 35, hitting .282 with 10 triples. Snider led the team in slugging percentage with a .562 pace in 85 games, and Moon, Howard, Fairly, and rookie Gordy Windhorn (in 34 games) also slugged over .500. Windhorn, retired as an executive with a Virginia beer distributor, told us,

"I had the wonderful experience to be with the Dodgers for a short time in 1961. I can recall that Johnny Podres was a battler on the mound and held his own with teammates Drysdale and Koufax. I remember that we could always expect 100 percent when Johnny was on the mound. I wish that I could have spent more time as a teammate of Johnny's."

Chapter Ten
The Dodgers 'Big Three'

In the October 1961 expansion draft, Craig was selected by the New York Mets, along with Hodges. In December, the Mets also acquired Neal from the Dodgers for Lee Walls and cash. The 1962 Mets roster included a few other former Dodgers as well: Zimmer, Pignatano, Labine, and Willard Hunter. The other National League expansion team, the Houston Colt .45's, drafted Larker, Farrell, Jim Golden and Bob Aspromonte from the Dodgers.

Beginning the 1962 season, the Brooklyn-to-Los Angeles transformation was nearly complete. The only remaining Brooklyn Dodgers hitters were Snider, Gilliam, and Roseboro (who played only 35 games in Brooklyn). Koufax, Drysdale, Podres, and Roebuck were the only pitchers who could be traced back to the Brooklyn era. The new Dodgers were built on pitching and speed.

"Willie Davis and Maury Wills were both incredibly fast," Johnny recalled.

"They would race the 60-yard dash, and Wills would pull ahead early. But Davis would get going and end up beating Wills by a step. Willie always used to run through third-base coach Pete Reiser's signs, and early in his career nearly always pulled the ball to second. One afternoon, Bavasi told him,

"'I'll pay you $25 for every ball you hit to shortstop.'

"Willie was so confident that he could do that every time up, he already had the $100 spent. But he ended up pulling them all to second anyway," Podres remembered.

Podres also recalled that Davis loved betting on horses with him and with Sherry.

"Willie once bet $700 on the number three horse, because Willie's nickname was 'Three-dog,'" recalled Johnny. (Willie's uniform number was three).

Podres advised him:

"Willie, if you really like that horse, for three hundred more bucks, you can buy it." The horse was for sale for $1,000.

By spring training 1962, the already excellent Dodger pitching assumed legendary status. Podres, after one of his best seasons in 1961, received a raise to $35,000. Future Hall of Fame members Koufax and Drysdale blossomed, becoming baseball's greatest 1-2 punch. Yet, Stan Williams recalled that Podres was still the leader of the Dodger staff. Williams, who still follows "the hell out of baseball" as an advance scout for the Tampa Bay Devil Rays, stated that,

"Podres was a tremendous pitcher and great competitor. And he threw hard. But 92 miles per hour didn't seem that fast compared to Drysdale, Koufax, and myself, when we were all around 100 mph."

Williams has fond memories of Podres and his years with the Dodgers.

"First of all I love Johnny Podres," Williams said.

"We were close, had many good times together, and I loved the great competitor that he was on the mound. Johnny was a great 'money-pitcher'—the bigger the game, the tougher he was. That showed up in the 1955 World Series, plus many other times. I don't feel Johnny receives the proper credit for his abilities. In today's society, if you weren't a Hall-of-Famer, you don't count. I have many stories of and about John—unfortunately most can't be put in print!"

Larry (Possum) Burright, a rookie in 1962, and today a carpenter still working in the construction industry, remembered that,

"Johnny was a very good pitcher, with excellent abilities, and I'd much rather have him on my team than against me. But I don't think he got a lot of credit because of Koufax and Drysdale. Johnny was a character (good that is), nice guy and good friend. I was a rookie in '62 and he treated me just like I'd been there a long time. The kind of guy you want on your team. Never had a bad word to say about anybody. If you can't get along with Johnny you can't get along with anybody."

Ken McMullen played for the Dodgers from 1962 to '64 and again from 1973 to '75. Today, he is a member of the Dodgers Speakers Bureau. His memories echo Burright's:

"John competed with a fiery passion to win. He was great to play behind because he knew how to pitch and didn't mess around on the mound. Off the field, he was a free spirit, and I wouldn't tell some of the stories. Being a youngster when I played with John, one thing he taught you was to be a class person. Johnny Podres was a class person. If you were a Dodger, you had to have class and John made sure you understood how it worked. Besides, sometimes he made sure the rookies got some of his leftover women. A great teammate and a better person."

Ken Rowe, who pitched for the Dodgers in 1963, and became a major league pitching coach for the Baltimore Orioles, remembered Johnny as "The Stopper."

"It seemed any time we lost a couple in a row, Johnny would pitch and end the losing streak," Rowe said.

"Johnny always wore a suit and tie the day he pitched—just in case he won—and he would go out and celebrate a little. And he never forgot a phone number."

Back in the early 1960s, Podres said about Don Drysdale:

"There's nobody close to him in a big game. He's the best I've seen since I've been in baseball. Sandy Koufax can do amazing things. There are nights that you can't believe it. But there are a few times when Sandy has trouble loosening up. You have to worry about him being right. With Drysdale, you never worry. You know."

Today, Johnny believes that Koufax was the greatest pitcher he ever saw.

"Koufax always had the talent. But after he started throwing strikes, during Spring Training in 1961, it was all over. For the next six years, he was the best pitcher who ever lived," Podres said.

In remembering Koufax and Drysdale, Johnny recalled an incident where they all ended up laughing together, at Podres' expense. In Chicago, Drysdale arranged dates for himself and Johnny, even though Podres was slated to pitch the next day. Alston liked to keep his eye on Johnny and make sure he didn't stay out too late, especially before a scheduled start. The next day, Alston confronted Podres in front of Koufax, Drysdale, and a few other players.

"You were out on a date last night, weren't you, Johnny?"

Podres replied, "No Walt, I didn't have a date last night."

"Alston stated, 'I know you did, because I've got the room next to you.' Okay, okay, I admit it," said Johnny.

"So, Alston turned to Drysdale and said, 'Don, are you all right to start today?'

Drysdale said, 'Sure, Walt,' and got the start. Koufax knew about Drysdale's date and was rolling around on the floor laughing," recalled Johnny.

During the early '60s, Koufax, Drysdale and Podres were known collectively as the Dodgers "Big Three," appearing together on Topps Baseball Card number 412 in the 1963 series. Although Johnny didn't make the Hall of Fame, since 1955 he showed the Dodgers how to win. As the acknowledged leader of the Dodgers' pitching staff in the early '60s, he blazed a path for Koufax and Drysdale. Early in his career, Podres received a few pointers from one of Brooklyn's first pitching legends, Dazzy Vance, and later worked with both Ramon and Pedro Martinez. No other pitcher in Dodgers' history linked the Brooklyn past with the Los Angeles future as did Podres. More important, in 1955, he dispatched the Bums from Brooklyn, and they have never been found in L.A.

Damn Giants

On April 10, 1962, Dodger Stadium opened in Chavez Ravine. Due to a drought, the grass was a brownish color, but Hollywood director Mervyn LeRoy (the king of the 1930s gangster film) gave O'Malley an idea: paint it with green vegetable dye. Johnny Podres, after his staff-best 18-5 performance the year before, won the honor of starting the first game, against the 1961 National League champion Reds, before 52,564 fans. The "First Lady of the Dodgers," Kay O'Malley, threw the ceremonial first pitch to Roseboro, and Latina diva Alma Pedroza sang the National Anthem. Unfortunately, the Reds' first batter, Eddie Kasko, ruined the celebration by doubling off Podres. And it was worse from there, as the Reds won 6-3, on a three-run, seventh-inning blast by Wally Post that soared between the two flagpoles in center field, scoring Vada Pinson and Frank Robinson. It was the first home run at Dodger Stadium, and Podres was lifted in favor of Sherry.

As of mid-May, the Dodgers were four games behind the Giants, but by the end of the month, a 12-game winning streak put them one-half game behind San Francisco, with a 34-15 record. By June, the Dodgers moved into first place.

On June 30, Koufax pitched the first of his four no-hitters (the last one a perfect game) against the New York Mets, 5-0. He struck out the first three batters (Richie Ashburn, Rod Kanehl and Felix Mantilla) on nine pitches. As July ended, the Dodgers put together a nine-game winning streak that included a three-game sweep of the Giants. Podres won one of the games, 3-1, behind a three-run homer by Howard.

Johnny Podres

With a sore shoulder and stiff neck, Johnny got off to a rough start, compiling a 4-7 record as of June 28. But on July 2nd, in the first game of a doubleheader, Johnny tied a modern National League record with eight consecutive strikeouts. He defeated Philadelphia 5–1, retiring the first 20 Phillies before Ted Savage singled. Williams won the second game 4–0, and the Dodgers moved into first place. Johnny then won six of his next seven decisions, which came at a crucial time, as Koufax was sidelined for two months with a rare circulation problem in the index finger of his pitching hand, "Reynaud's Phenomenon." But on August 10, in the first of three games with the Giants at Candlestick Park, Billy O'Dell defeated Podres and the Dodgers, 11-2, cutting the Dodger lead to four games.

In mid-September, the Dodgers completed a seven-game winning streak, and maintained a four-game lead over the Giants. Then, mired in a hitting slump, they collapsed during the last two weeks of the season, winning only three of 13 games, while the Giants won five of their last seven.

On September 26, Wills stole his 100th base and Howard drove in five runs, as Johnny (in his 250th major league start) shut down the Houston Colt .45's 13-1. The Dodgers' magic number stood at three with three games left to play, all against St. Louis. On September 28, the Dodgers lost to the Cardinals in 10 innings 3-2, with Perranoski taking the loss. Drysdale, who pitched over 300 innings in '62, lost to the Cardinals and Ernie Broglio the next day, 2-0. Two unearned runs scored on Howard's dropped fly ball off the bat of Dal Maxvill.

On September 30, Johnny's 30th birthday, the Dodgers kept a one-game lead over the Giants, with one game left for each team. Podres, who had won eight of his last nine decisions in St. Louis, held the Cardinal scoreless into the eighth inning, allowing only two singles. Curt Simmons also manacled the Dodgers for eight innings. In fact, the Dodgers had not scored in 20 straight innings.

In the bottom of the eighth with one out and a 1-2 count, St. Louis catcher Gene Oliver whacked Podres' pitch deep into the seats between the foul pole and the visiting bullpen.

"I pitched the best game of my life," Podres said.

"Even the pitch to Oliver was a good one, a curve in tight."

The Dodgers lost 1-0, while the Giants beat the Colts 2-1. The heartbreaking loss forced only the fourth playoff in National League history, all of which involved the Dodgers (1946, 1951, 1959, and 1962). Remaining upbeat, Podres told the *Los Angeles Times*,

"We won a playoff three years ago, so why in the hell can't we again."

Despite being tied with the Giants, it had been a groundbreaking season for the Dodgers. Wills broke Ty Cobb's record by stealing 104 bases. He batted .299 with 208 hits and 130 runs scored, capturing the National League's Most Valuable Player award. Tommy Davis led the league in batting (.346), hits (230) and runs batted in (153, the highest total since 1949), with 27 home runs.

Howard smacked 31 homers, knocked in 119 runners, and slugged .560. Willie Davis hit 21 homers, 10 triples, stole 32 bases, and batted .285 in his second full season. Fairly cracked 14 homers and established a solid .379 on-base percentage. In 45 games, Doug Camilli (son of former Brooklyn Dodger Dolf Camilli) slugged .523 and posted a .366 on-base percentage, both impressive for a back-up catcher. Snider played his last season for the Dodgers, hitting .278 with five home runs. Sold for $40,000, he would join several former Dodgers on the 1963 New York Mets.

Johnny Podres finished the season at 15-13, with a 3.81 earned-run average, and 178 strikeouts (sixth best in the league and his highest single-season total). It marked the seventh time he was in the National League's top ten in strikeouts per nine innings, with 6.28. He proved extremely durable, starting 40 games (second best in the league), and pitching 255 innings. He also started the second 1962 All-Star game, which the American League won 9-4.

Drysdale completed his finest season, with a 25-9 record, 314 innings pitched, 2.83 ERA, and 232 strikeouts. He won the Cy Young Award and finished fifth in the National League MVP voting. He led the league in victories, innings pitched, and strikeouts. Despite injuries, Koufax turned in another brilliant season, winning 14 and losing 7, with 216 strikeouts and a 2.54 earned-run average. Williams also won 14 games, losing 12, and compiling a 4.46 ERA. Roebuck (10-2, 119 innings, 3.09 ERA, and nine saves), Perranoski (20 saves) and Sherry (11 saves) led the bullpen.

The 1962 Giants featured a powerful offense and pretty good pitching. They led the league in hitting (.278) and home runs (204). Willie Mays led the league with 49 home runs, hitting .304 with 141 RBIs, and a .615 slugging percentage. He was followed by Orlando Cepeda (.306, 35, 114), Willie McCovey (.293, 20, 54), Felipe Alou (.316, 25, 98), and Harvey Kuenn (.304, 10, 68). The starting pitchers were Billy O'Dell (19-14, 3.53 ERA), Jack Sanford (24-7, 3.43 ERA), Juan Marichal (18-11, 3.36 ERA), and Billy Pierce (16-6, 3.49 ERA). Stu Miller and Dodgers nemesis Don Larsen manned the bullpen, with 19 and 11 saves, respectively.

On October 1, the Dodgers and Giants met in San Francisco for the first playoff game. Giants manager Alvin Dark, "The Swamp Fox," ordered the ground crew to soak the basepaths to deter Wills, which proved unnecessary. Pierce threw a three-hitter and beat Koufax, 8-0, on four homers, including two by Mays.

In the second game, in Los Angeles, Drysdale went against Sanford. Down 5-0 in the sixth, after a scoreless streak of 35 innings, the Dodgers scored seven runs on hits by Snider, Howard, Camilli and Walls. San Francisco came back to tie the game in the eighth, but the Dodgers won in the ninth, 8-7, on three walks and Fairly's sacrifice fly.

Juan Marichal was set to face Podres (pitching on two days' rest) in the rubber game, October 3, 1962. A Dodger Stadium crowd of 45,693 fans expected a very tense match-up. In the third inning, the Giants scored two runs off Podres, including one that was unearned. The Dodgers committed three errors, including one by Podres, when he threw Marichal's bunted ball into centerfield, trying to nail Jose Pagan at second. But Johnny got out of the inning when Cepeda hit into a double play.

The Dodgers got a run back in the fourth (Snider scored on a ground ball by Howard), and took the lead in the sixth on a single by Snider and a two-run homer by Tommy Davis. In the seventh, Wills singled, stole second and third, and scored on catcher Ed Bailey's wild throw.

Going into the ninth inning, it was 4-2 Dodgers, with Ed Roebuck (having the best season of his career), on the mound. Roebuck was brought into the game in the sixth inning, already having pitched five innings in the previous two playoff games. He pitched brilliantly in the sixth, retiring the side after Podres left the game with the bases loaded and nobody out.

In the ninth, Roebuck yielded a pinch single to Matty Alou, and retired Harvey Kuenn on a force play (which should have been a double play, but second baseman Larry Burright was playing too far away). He walked McCovey and Felipe Alou to load the bases. Mays then followed with an infield single, and it was 4-3 Los Angeles, with one out and the bases loaded. Podres recounted what happened next:

"Alston sent in Stan Williams, who hadn't pitched in ten days. Roebuck had been pitching well, but he got tired. Several players suggested to Alston that he bring in Drysdale, who offered to pitch, but Alston told him,

'You're pitching against the Yankees tomorrow in the World Series.'"

In the dugout, Durocher fed the fires, demanding that Alston bring in Drysdale. According to Wills, Alston didn't use Drysdale simply because it was Durocher's idea.

After the game, Drysdale stated,

"You're damn right I would have liked to pitch. Only they didn't ask me."

Williams retired Cepeda on a long sacrifice fly that tied the game. He then threw a wild pitch, intentionally walked Ed Bailey to load the bases, and unintentionally walked Jim Davenport to force in the go-ahead run. Perranoski relieved Williams, but the Giants scored another run on a grounder by Pagan that was fumbled by Burright. It was Williams' last appearance for the Dodgers—he was traded to the Yankees in the off-season for Bill (Moose) Skowron.

Dark brought in Pierce to relieve for the Giants and he retired Wills, Gilliam, and Walls in order. The Giants won, 6-4, and Larsen got the victory. San Francisco scored four runs on two singles, four walks, and an error. The most disastrous game in the history of the Los Angeles Dodgers had just unfolded.

After the game, Johnny Podres recalled,

"Tommy Davis followed Alston around saying,

'You stole my money.'"

The team was upset, and began drinking the whiskey and champagne that was in the clubhouse for the "victory party," and Alston retreated to his office. It was a shame, because the 1962 Dodgers were a great team that might have been able to beat the Yankees in the World Series, which the Giants failed to do. The Dodgers won 102 games against 63 losses, again leading the league in attendance (2,755,184) in their first season at Dodger Stadium.

Pitching against the Mets on July 10, 1963 at the Polo Grounds. Johnny extended the Mets' losing streak to 11 games with a three-hit, 1-0 shutout. Batterymate John Roseboro homered for the Dodgers.

Bob, John and Robert S. Bennett

Johnny receives advice from Sandy Koufax prior to Game Two of the 1963 World Series on October 3, 1963. In Game One, Sandy set a record by striking out 15 Yankees. After Johnny's 4-1 triumph, Mickey Mantle said, "Podres is not as fast as Sandy Koufax but he's just as good."

Johnny Podres

1999 Dodgers "Heroes" patch honoring Podres.

1963 Topps Baseball Card, Dodgers' Big Three, with Podres, Don Drysdale and Sandy Koufax.

Bob, John and Robert S. Bennett

Wedding at St. Colman's Catholic Church, Ardmore, Pennsylvania, February 12, 1966.

Johnny Podres

Johnny pictured in Dodger Stadium near the end of his Los Angeles career. (Johnny Podres' personal collection).

Traded to the Detroit Tigers, Johnny warms up for Manager Charlie Dressen before a May 10, 1966 game with the Cleveland Indians. Dressen, who taught Podres his famous "pull the shade down" change-up in 1953, suffered a heart attack less than a week later and died on August 10th.

Bob, John and Robert S. Bennett

Souvenir photo as a coach with the San Diego Padres in 1973. Johnny's staff included Randy Jones, Clay Kirby, and Fred Norman. Don Zimmer managed the team to a 60-102 record.

As the pitching coach for the Minnesota Twins in the early 1980s. (Photo by J.D. McCarthy).

Actor Jack Nicholson (a Yankee fan) and Johnny at Dodger Stadium in the early 1990s. Nicholson asked to meet Podres, the only Brooklyn pitcher to defeat the Yankees in a final World Series game. Photo courtesy Johnny Podres.

A statue of Johnny Podres at the Baseball Hall of Fame in Cooperstown, New York. The plaque reads: "The Pitcher: Johnny Podres, 1998, Cast Bronze, by Stanley Bleifeld."

Another view of "The Pitcher." Campy is behind the plate....

Johnny Podres

Podres demonstrates how he grips a fastball

Curveball

The "Pull the Shade Down" Change-up. Note that his fingers are off the ball.

Bob, John and Robert S. Bennett

John Bennett interviews Johnny Podres.

Clockwise from top left, Joan, Johnny, Johnny and Joey.

Johnny Podres

Joan and Johnny Podres and their dog, Andre, pictured in front of their upstate New York home in 2004.

Joan and Johnny with the 1955 Sports Illustrated "Sportsman of the Year" award.

Bob, John and Robert S. Bennett

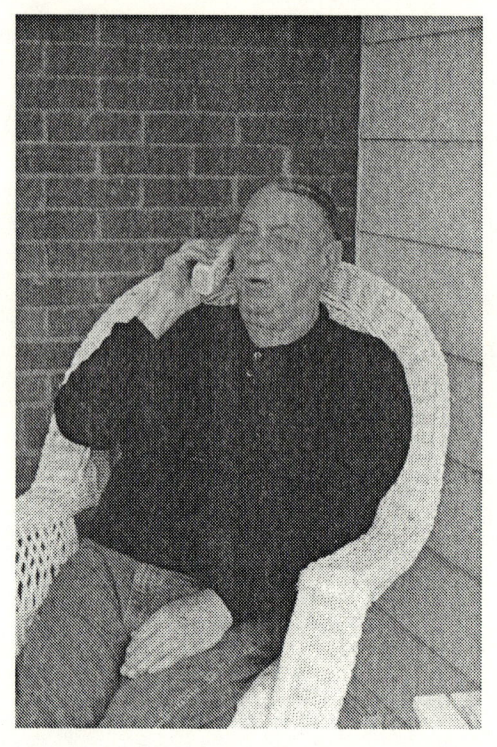

Johnny enjoys catching up with former teammates and friends, and spends most mornings on the phone.

Podres' New York License Plate.

Chapter Eleven
Bring on the Yankees

During and after the 1962 season, rumors flew that Durocher would replace Alston as manager.

"In early 1963, O'Malley wanted to fire Alston," Johnny remembered, "but Alston called Bavasi, who supported him, back to Los Angeles. Buzzie made a stand and said,

'If you make Durocher the manager, you no longer have a GM.'"

Durocher responded to charges that he was actively seeking Alston's job, stating that the people who believe these rumors "must be smoking the kind of cigarettes without any printing on them." Sid Ziff, writing in the *Los Angeles Times*, speculated that Alston, Durocher and Becker would be gone and that Pete Reiser, who was popular with the younger players, would be named the Dodgers' new manager for the '63 season. But O'Malley and Bavasi stuck with Alston and the same coaching staff from 1962, including Leo the Lip.

Early in the season, one of the more famous Alston episodes may have ignited the team. On May 6, the Dodgers lost a double-header to Pittsburgh and were languishing in seventh place. The team was traveling to the airport in an old bus. It was hot and humid, and the players began yelling and complaining to traveling secretary Lee Scott. Podres remembers that Roebuck was one of the more vocal Dodgers. Meanwhile, the Pirates went flying past the Dodgers in a brand-new, air-conditioned bus on their way out of town for a road trip. Alston gradually became very upset about the players' complaints and ordered the bus to pull over. According to Podres, Alston said,

"Any son of a bitch that doesn't like the bus should step forward." But nobody did, and the rest of the ride was quiet. Wills described the incident as a turning point, stating,

"We got real hot after that." Johnny Podres recalled,

"After it was all said and done, we *did* get a better bus."

Roebuck would soon be traded to the Washington Senators, where Hodges had recently become the manager. Roebuck stated that the trade, specifically getting away from Alston, was "like getting out of prison."

Sportswriter Dick Young wrote in the *New York Daily News* on April 13, that several Dodgers were critical of Alston, including Koufax, Sherry and Podres. The source of the criticism, according to Young, was that Alston was a tough disciplinarian who kept a tight rein on the players. Reportedly, Alston suspended beer drinking on team flights and conducted late-night bed checks. Young concluded his article by stating that Alston, a fighter, would never go quietly.

"Alston isn't going to quit, ever. He may get fired, or more accurately, assassinated."

On May 8, O'Malley told reporters,

"Walter Alston is my manager and I have no intention of making a change."

Alston continued to manage the Dodgers into the 1976 season, was elected to the Hall of Fame in 1983, and died in 1984. Durocher continued as a coach through the 1964 season, becoming the manager of the Chicago Cubs in 1966.

Off to another rocky start in 1963, Johnny suffered with a sore elbow and was treated by Dr. Kerlan. He won his first game (after two losses) on April 24, shutting out the Reds, 7-0, propelled by Howard, Fairly, and Roseboro home runs. Johnny then missed a couple of starts with a sore shoulder.

On May 11, Koufax threw his second no-hitter, beating the Giants at Dodger Stadium, 8-0. Podres won his second game on May 16 on another shutout, 1-0, against Pittsburgh. And on May 21, Podres pitched a complete game and struck out 10, beating the Mets 4-2, for the Dodgers' seventh straight win. On June 12, John beat the Colts, 9-1, and the Dodgers moved into first place by percentage points, having won 15 of their last 19 games.

On July 1, Johnny beat the Braves. 2-1. He fanned 12, and brought his record to 5-6. The next day, Drysdale shut out the Cardinals 1-0, and the Dodgers moved back into first place. They would stay there for the rest of the season.

Podres threw his third career two-hitter on July 5th against the Reds (he had two others in 1959). Allowing singles only to Johnny Edwards and Tommy Harper, Podres won, 1-0, on a home run by Howard. In his next start, on July 10, he beat the Mets 1-0, for his fourth shutout of the season, improving his record to 7-6. Johnny had another two-hitter going until Ron Hunt singled in the ninth. He whiffed 11 Mets. The Dodgers scored their only run on a homer by Roseboro. Podres appeared to have fully recovered from the sore elbow that plagued him earlier in the season.

John went the distance on July 14, beating the Phillies, 3-2, although the game was called for rain after the sixth inning. On July 23, he went back into shutout mode, blanking the Pirates, 6-0 (his fifth shutout of the season and sixth consecutive victory), bringing his record to 10-6. A five-run Dodger eighth inning was capped by McMullen's two-run homer. But on July 27, the Phils beat Podres at home for the first time since September 21, 1957, and his record fell to 10-7.

On a sweltering day in Houston, August 4, 1963, Podres had a no-hitter spoiled in the ninth inning. Johnny Temple hit a curveball just out of the reach of second-baseman Marv Breeding (recently acquired from the Senators for Roebuck). Larry Dierker, who pitched for the Colts and the Astros from 1964-1976, recalls hearing from a teammate that,

"It was so hot at Colt Stadium that day. Podres gave up his first hit to open the ninth. He then took himself out of the game. It was so hot that he wasn't motivated by the shutout. If he couldn't pitch a no-hitter, he wanted out of there."

Sherry came in to relieve and the Dodgers won, 4-0. Podres added a two-run double to support his pitching efforts.

On August 13, 42-year-old Warren Spahn set the all-time strikeout record against Podres and the Dodgers with 2,383 (two more than Rube Waddell). The Braves won 4-3, and Bob Miller (in relief of Podres) took the loss. Interestingly, Koufax (who retired at 30) finished with more strikeouts (2,396) than Spahn had accumulated at age 42.

Three days later, the Dodgers defeated the Mets, 9-7. While Podres did not get the win (which went to reliever Ron Perranoski, having an incredible season), Johnny slugged his second career home run, a two-run shot against former teammate, Roger Craig. Podres' first home run came in 1962 off Pittsburgh's Al McBean.

The Dodgers defeated the Cardinals, 7-5, on August 20, extending their lead to 6½ games, another no-decision for Podres. He then lost to the Braves 2-1, and to the Reds 9-5, falling to 11-10 as August ended. Near the end of August, Johnny suffered a stiff neck "while diving into a swimming pool in an unusual way." He told Alston about it, and Walt was "pissed off," because, according to Podres,

"He thought I got the stiff neck while engaged in some sort of amorous activity."

"That day," Johnny said, "Alston didn't let me start, but I was brought into a game in the ninth inning and picked up a save. I got the start in the second game of a double-header the next day, but after that, Alston didn't start me for 10 days."

Podres got the save in a 5-3 victory on September 1st against the Giants, retiring Jose Pagan, Felipe Alou, and Willie Mays in order. The next day, Johnny beat the Colts 7-1, raising his record to 12-10.

Six days later, Johnny was used in relief of Drysdale for two innings in a 5-3 loss to the Giants, and again on September 8th in relief of Bob Miller, for two-thirds of an inning—a 5-4 loss to the Giants.

Jim Murray wrote in the *Los Angeles Times* that Alston's decision to use Podres in relief "has put such a serious crimp in John's social life." Murray wrote that,

"John, for years, has had a fairly uncomplicated social life. He pitched every fourth day." According to Murray, the relief role did not suit Podres.

"Johnny is a money pitcher, a stakes horse, not a plater," Murray wrote.

Johnny was playing poker in the back of the Dodger jet, as the team flew to Pittsburgh on September 12. Alston asked Podres to come down the aisle.

"Are you okay to pitch today, John?"

"Yes I am, Walt, but how do you think Drysdale will feel if we pass by his turn?"

Podres started and beat the Pirates 5-3, on a first-inning grand slam by Roseboro. There were weather reports of a storm approaching Pittsburgh. Johnny worked fast and furiously to get five innings in. He completed the task in 60 minutes flat, 15 minutes before the storm was due. But the storm never came. Podres went seven innings and Perranoski worked the final two. Johnny's record stood at 13-10.

On a flight to St. Louis on September 15, Johnny was again playing poker in the back of the plane, and Alston asked to see him.

"You okay to pitch tomorrow?" Alston asked. "I want you to pitch tomorrow against St. Louis."

Al Ferrara is a former Brooklyn high school student (who graduated with Joe Pepitone, Joe Torre, and Bob Aspromonte). He has been a Carnegie Hall pianist and a television and movie actor. He appeared on *Gilligan's Island*, playing a "native" alongside fellow Dodger Jim Lefebvre, and on three episodes of *Batman* as a henchmen of one of the show's various celebrity villains, including silent-screen actress Tallulah Bankhead as "Black Widow." He was called up from Spokane mid-way through the 1963 season, and assigned as Podres' new roommate. Ferrara remembered:

"Podres was in Alston's doghouse toward the end of the year. We were eight games in front but then the tough Cardinals won 19 out of 20 and although we were playing great our lead shrank to one game with a week to go and we were going to St. Louis to play three. After each Cardinal win, the great Harry Caray would sing 'the Cardinals are coming, tra la la. The Cardinals are coming, tra la la.' Alston went to Johnny and told him he was pitching the first game. Drysdale came to me and told me,

'Make sure he gets his rest.'

"John and I were both nocturnal animals. As soon as we hit the room, he says to me,

'Where are we going?'

"I said, 'You're going to bed!' He did and he pitched seven brilliant innings of one-run ball. We swept the series. As we left St. Louis we said, 'The Cardinals are going tra la la, tra la la.'"

It was 100 degrees in St. Louis on September 16th, as Podres took the mound in front of 32,442 fans. He retired the first 16 batters, until Tim McCarver singled in the sixth, and the Dodgers led, 1-0. In the seventh, Stan Musial hit his 475th career homer, tying the game at 1-1. But Podres regained his poise, pitching to only three batters in the eighth. The Dodgers got two runs in the ninth on hits by Fairly, Willie Davis, and Moose Skowron (pinch hitting for Podres). Perranoski finished the game, retiring Dick Groat, Musial and Ken Boyer. Giving up just three hits, Podres (14-10) beat Bobby Shantz in relief of Ernie Broglio 3-1.

The next day, Koufax pitched his 11th shutout, and the Dodgers won 4-0, on a two-run homer by Howard, off the right field roof, in the eighth. Pete Richert faced Bob Gibson in the third game. After seven innings, the score was 5-1 in favor of St. Louis. But the Dodgers scored three runs in the eighth to cut the lead to 5-4. In the ninth inning against Ron Taylor, Dodgers rookie Dick Nen (who had just been called up from Spokane), hit a home run to deep right center field, tying the game at five. Finally, in the 13th inning, Willie Davis scored on a bases-loaded ground ball by Maury Wills for the go-ahead run. Perranoski closed out the Cardinals in the bottom of the 13th, and the Dodgers won 6-5.

Although the Cardinals looked like favorites heading in to the series, especially after what had happened in 1962, afterward the Cardinals were four games out with only nine to play. Drysdale made it official, on September 24, defeating the Mets in Los Angeles 4-1. Johnny shouted to reporters:

"No playoffs this year!"

The Cardinals finished six games out, and the Dodgers went on to win the World Series, sweeping the Yankees in four straight games. It was Johnny Podres' last superstar season.

A Chip in His Shoulder

During spring training in 1964, Johnny pulled a muscle in his arm while snapping off a curve to Albie Pearson. The injury delayed the start of his season, but Podres was back in action by April 25, against Spahn in Milwaukee. Spahn hit him in the elbow, setting loose a bone chip. In his second start, in mid-May, Johnny couldn't pitch his way out of the first inning against Pittsburgh. Podres had considerable pain in his arm, which felt "like 100 hot needles jabbing my elbow."

On May 18, it was announced that Podres would probably have to undergo surgery, although Dr. Kerlan would continue to evaluate the situation. Kerlan stated that,

"The bone chip has been there apparently for some time."

The Dodgers considered letting Podres make his next scheduled start against the Mets, but decided to wait for Kerlan's prognosis. In the last week of May, as the Dodgers prepared for a 14-game road trip, they decided to leave Johnny in Los Angeles. Podres told the *Los Angeles Times*:

"I'm not finished. I'm only 31. If it has to be surgery, let's do it. Let's do it right now. I don't want to waste any more time."

After Podres' unsuccessful attempts to pitch to coach Becker on June 8, it was decided that surgery was the only option. On June 11th at Daniel Freeman Hospital in Inglewood, doctors removed a pea-sized chip. Dr. Kerlan described the condition as an "unplaced bone" in Podres' left elbow and proclaimed,

"I would say John will be extremely fortunate if he is able to pitch this season."

The Dodgers brought up Howie Reed to replace Podres, and during the year auditioned several other young pitchers, including Joe Moeller, John Purdin, and Bill Singer (who pitched a no-hitter and won 20 games for the Dodgers in 1969). Purdin, who today is semi-retired and recently re-located to Myrtle Beach, South Carolina, recalled,

"Johnny had great control, and an outstanding change-up. His ability to keep batters off stride was excellent. He showed me that you don't have to be over-powering to get hitters out. Johnny had a great sense of humor, and was a great guy to have on any team. He was always up-beat and made you laugh."

With injuries to Podres, Koufax, and Drysdale, the Dodgers collapsed, finishing in seventh place, with an 80-82 record. Podres was 0-2 in two and 2/3 innings, for a 16.88 earned-run average. Koufax was 19-5, with a sparkling 1.74 earned-run average in 29 games. Drysdale, who missed time near the end of the season, went 18-16, with a 2.18 ERA.

Other than Drysdale and Koufax, the Dodger starting rotation was lackluster. Moeller, Larry Miller (who pitched for the Dodgers only for the '64 season), and Phil Ortega balanced out the rotation, with Perranoski, Bob Miller, Reed, and newcomer Jim Brewer in the bullpen. Dodger offense also declined. Howard clubbed 24 homers, but hit only .226. Willie Davis hit .294 with 42 stolen bases, and Maury Wills stole 53 bases and hit .275. Rookies Wes Parker, Jeff Torborg, and 17-year-old Willie Crawford (who passed away in 2004) joined the Dodgers.

During winter '64, Podres pitched in the Arizona Instructional League. He steadily regained his arm strength, and felt loose at the end of the season. Meanwhile, on December 4, the Dodgers traded Howard, McMullen, Ortega, Richert, and 1963 hero Dick Nen to the Washington Senators for Claude Osteen, John Kennedy, and $100,000 in cash. Osteen, who became a successful major league pitching coach, recalled Johnny being very helpful when he joined the Dodgers.

"Johnny was a very good pitcher and had probably the best change-up in the majors in his time," said Osteen, now a consultant for the Arizona Diamondbacks who watches "every game that time permits."

"Johnny was a great teacher of the change as well as other facets of pitching, and a good pitching coach. I learned several key points about teaching and throwing the change-up from him. I also remember him going to the racetrack, whether it was horses or dogs it was a real joy for him. He made a lot of people laugh and also relax in the course of a pressure-packed season."

An Engaging Comeback

A March 2, 1965, *United Press International* report said,

"Johnny Podres was on the mound almost as long today as he was during the entire 1964 season and the progress report from Dodgers manager Walter Alston was highly optimistic. After Podres pitched 10 minutes of batting practice, Alston said he was 'very pleased'."

On March 7, Johnny pitched two innings, giving up one run in an intra-squad game, as Coach Danny Ozark's team defeated Coach Preston Gomez's team, 3-2. On March 29, he pitched a scoreless inning against the Baltimore Orioles to complete a Dodger victory that snapped the Orioles' five-game winning streak. Overall, Podres enjoyed some of his best spring training pitching performances.

The Dodgers shook up their coaching staff for the 1965 season. Gone were Becker, Mulleavy, Reiser, and Durocher. The new coaches were Gomez, Ozark, Lefty Phillips, and Jim Gilliam (a player-coach during the 1965 and 1966 seasons, who served as a full-time coach until his death in 1978). Gomez, who played in eight games for the 1944 Washington Senators and managed three major league teams in seven seasons, told us,

"Podres was a money pitcher. When you needed to win he was one of the best. As the late Walter Alston used to say, John will get the ball if we need to win. He had the best change-up that I have ever seen, kept the club loose, and was a very smart, great teammate. I knew when he pitched for six or seven innings we had a chance to win. He kept you in the game."

On April 23, Podres shut the Phillies out, 4-0, with a four-hit, complete game, with the only solid hit by Richie Allen. It was Podres' first victory since beating the Yankees in the 1963 World Series. Bavasi told the *Los Angeles Times*,

"Dr. Kerlan didn't send me a bill for Johnny's operation. I guess he wanted to wait and see how Johnny did first. But whatever the fee is, it'll be worth it."

Podres followed with another victory on May 6 against the second-place Reds, 4-3, behind Ron Fairly's homer off Joe Nuxhall. Podres' arm started to stiffen in the sixth, however, and he was relieved by Bob Miller.

On May 10, the Dodgers beat Houston in 10 innings, 3-2. Podres pitched nine innings, giving up only two runs (and knocking in one of the Dodgers' runs), but left while the game was still tied.

He pitched another complete game victory on May 27, 3-2 over Milwaukee, improving his record to 3-0 with a 1.60 ERA. The Dodgers won in the ninth as Podres' roomie, Ferrara, walked with the bases loaded. On June 5, Podres suffered his first loss of the season, 9-1, to Milwaukee. He gave up five earned runs in six innings, four on a grand slam by Mack Jones.

Richie Allen hit a 500-foot home run off Podres on June 10, leading the Phillies to a 4-0 victory and bringing Johnny's record to 3-2. Allen's bomb flew out of the stadium 100 feet high, striking a car across the street. It was Podres' 100th career loss.

Four days later, Johnny was used in relief of Nick Willhite, Miller and Perranoski against the Mets. He retired the last two hitters, Roy McMillan and Charlie Smith, on two pitches, preserving a 4-3 Dodger victory. But his record fell to 3-3 on his next start at Dodger Stadium, where he was bested by Chris Short and the Phillies, 4-2.

On June 27, he lost again, 10-2, to Pittsburgh. After the game, Pirate hitter Gene Freese compared the Dodger batting attack to "watching a silent movie." Although Podres was hammered in the Pittsburgh game, in most of his outings he received little run support from the weak-hitting Dodgers.

A few days later, on July 1, Podres took his fifth loss, as the Cubs beat the Dodgers, 6-3, on two home runs by Glenn Beckert, one against Podres. Johnny had problems with the Cubs, and hadn't beaten them in his last nine attempts—since August 30, 1961. After the loss, Alston apparently lost confidence in John, and Podres was used in relief for most of the rest of the season. But he won his fourth game and improved to 4-5, on July 26 against the Reds. The Dodgers, led by two-run homers from Willie Davis and Parker, won 5-4 to take a two-game lead in the pennant race.

Podres lost his last game for the Dodgers on August 16. The Phillies and Chris Short pasted L.A. 6-1, and John could not escape the third inning.

On August 21, in a two-inning relief appearance, Podres beat the Giants in the 11th inning, 6-4, on a two-run home run by Parker, as the Dodgers regained first place. He struck out the last two batters, Jesus Alou and Len Gabrielson. The next day featured the famous Roseboro-Juan Marichal incident.

"Koufax didn't like to throw at hitters," Johnny told us, "so Roseboro threw the ball close to Marichal's ear, and Marichal thought that Roseboro tried to hit him in the head. Marichal turned around and hit him with the bat. Roseboro was bleeding and the team was worried."

The ensuing 14-minute brawl was one of the most violent in baseball history.

Asked whether Drysdale, known for a fastball that seemed to come at right-handed hitters from third base, enjoyed throwing at hitters, Podres responded:

"Drysdale didn't like to throw at hitters, but he believed in protecting his teammates—they throw at one of our guys, we take out two of theirs. Today, players are concerned with their multi-million dollar value, as they should, so headhunting is no longer a part of the game."

On September 4, the Dodgers beat the Astros, 5-0, and Podres evened his record at six. He got the win in relief of Brewer, who made a rare start and pitched four innings. Drysdale and Perranoski completed the shutout. Five days later, on September 9, 1965, Koufax pitched his fourth no-hitter, a perfect game, against the Chicago Cubs. The Dodgers, managing only one hit off Bob Hendley, won 1-0. Watching from the dugout, Podres described Koufax's performance as "incredible" and stated that he "could not believe what he was seeing."

"In the ninth inning, he struck out the side on ten pitches and his hat came off six times," recalled Johnny.

With several crucial games remaining in the 1965 season, Alston gave Johnny an important assignment against the Reds on September 28. He pitched four shutout innings and the Dodgers had a comfortable lead, but pitching coach Lefty Phillips wanted to remove him in favor of Reed. Podres told him,

"Lefty, I know you don't like me, but I'm pitching another inning."

And he did, picking up the win, his final victory for the Dodgers. It was the Dodgers' 10th victory in a row, keeping them tied with the Giants. The final score was 6-1 Dodgers, led by two Willie Davis dingers.

The Dodgers clinched the pennant on the second-to-last game of the season, Saturday, October 2nd. Koufax defeated Milwaukee, 3-1, for the Dodgers' 14th victory in 15 games. On Sunday, Johnny arrived at Dodger Stadium hung over from the victory celebration. He felt lousy.

"You want to pitch two or three innings today and tune up for the World Series?" Phillips asked.

"Who the hell are you shittin', Lefty? I won't smell the World Series. You know I ain't pitching in the Series!"

After the National Anthem, Podres called out to third-base umpire Augie Donatelli (who worked right field in the seventh game of the 1955 World Series),

"Hey, Augie?"

"What do you say, John?"

"I say you're horseshit!"

The umpire responded with his thumb in the air.

"I say you're gone."

"So I told Phillips, I guess I ain't pitching today, Lefty. And then I went back to the hotel and resumed drinking."

The Dodgers finished the season at 97-65, two games ahead of the Giants, and first in attendance with 2,553,577. Johnny's 7-6 record belied a successful season. He appeared in 27 games and compiled a highly respectable 3.43 earned-run average. Koufax and Drysdale both had outstanding seasons. Koufax was 26-8, with a 2.04 ERA and a record 382 strikeouts, capturing the Cy Young Award and finishing second in the National League MVP race to Willie Mays. Drysdale won 23 and lost 12, with a 2.77 ERA.

Osteen pitched well, winning 15 games (against 15 losses), with a 2.79 ERA. In the bullpen, Perranoski, Miller, Reed, and Brewer all pitched solidly.

The Dodgers featured an all-switch-hitting infield, with Parker at first, rookie of the year Jim Lefebvre at second, Wills at short, and Gilliam at third. Lefebvre and Lou Johnson shared the team lead with 12 home runs. Maury Wills hit .286 and stole 94 bases. Wally Moon played his last season, hitting .202 in 53 games.

Without Howard, and a season-ending injury to Tommy Davis (after he appeared in only 17 games), the offense lacked power. No Dodger regular slugged over .400. Drysdale probably should have played every day, as he smacked seven homers, drove in 19 runs, hit .300 and slugged .508.

On October 5, 1965, the day before the World Series, Frank Finch of the *Los Angeles Times* reported:

"That well-known man about town, Johnny Podres, has decided to settle down. He is engaged to Miss Joan Taylor of Ardmore, Pennsylvania, a stunning member of the Ice Follies chorus line. They yet haven't set a nuptial date."

In the first game of the World Series, Sandy Koufax declined to pitch because of the Jewish holiday of Yom Kippur. Drysdale started, and the Minnesota Twins, led by Zoilo Versalles and Don Mincher, defeated the Dodgers, 8-2, at Metropolitan Stadium. Koufax pitched the second game and was defeated by Jim Kaat, 5-1.

But when the Series moved to Dodger Stadium on October 9, 1965, L.A. busted loose. In Game Three, Osteen pitched a complete game shutout, beating the Twins 4-0, before 55,934 fans. Behind Drysdale, the Dodgers won Game Four on home runs by Parker and Johnson, 7-2. And Koufax pitched a complete game shutout to win Game Five 7-0, as the light-hitting Dodgers collected 14 hits.

For Game Six, the teams returned to Metropolitan Stadium. Jim Grant pitched a complete game and homered, as the Twins won 5-1, setting the stage for the seventh game. Johnny Podres, who sat in the bullpen during the entire Series, recalled that Alston held a meeting before the game and said,

"'This is your World Series, so who do you want to pitch in Game Seven?' Everybody in the room said, 'the Super Jew.'"

Koufax received his nickname in conjunction with two other Jewish players on the ballclub, brothers Norm Sherry (the "Happy Jew") and Larry Sherry (the "Rude Jew").

In Game Seven, the Dodgers scored two runs in the fourth inning on a home run by Johnson, a double by Fairly, and a single by Parker. That proved sufficient, in a very tense game, as Koufax mastered the Twins with a complete-game shutout, yielding only three hits. In the bottom of the ninth, Koufax allowed a single to Harmon Killebrew with one out. But he struck out Earl Battey and Bob Allison to win the game. With a 2-1 record, a miniscule 0.38 ERA, and 29 strikeouts, Koufax was named Series MVP for the second time.

On February 12, 1966, Johnny and Joan were married in Pennsylvania. Later that year, on Tuesday, December 6, 1966, their first son, Joseph Michael Podres, was born (at 7 pounds, 7 ounces, at Daniel Freeman Hospital).

The Hold-Out and the Trade

Before Spring Training in 1966, Koufax and Drysdale began their famous joint holdout. The two stars asked for three-year contracts at $166,666 per year. When Bavasi and the Dodgers rejected the offers, Koufax and Drysdale refused to report to Spring Training. Arthur Daley wrote in the *New York Times* on March 16:

"He [Bavasi] is fighting off two things. One is a joint assault on Walter O'Malley's well-guarded treasury. The other is a three-year contract. As a matter of principle, if for no other reason, he cannot surrender. Pandora's Box must be kept padlocked."

One of the first steps towards the emancipation of the ballplayer, the hold-out was followed by Curt Flood's refusal to accept a 1970 trade to the Phillies, which led to his challenge of baseball's reserve clause in the U.S. Supreme Court.

On March 17, the *New York Times* reported that Koufax and Drysdale signed with Paramount Pictures to make *Warning Shot*, a crime drama to be directed by Buzz Kulik, and starring television's "Fugitive," David Janssen. Drysdale would play the part of a television commentator while Koufax was cast in the role of a detective sergeant. The film was released in 1967, but without Koufax and Drysdale. On March 30, 1966, they signed for $120,000 and $105,000, respectively.

Podres made an impressive spring debut on March 6, retiring six in a row in an intra-squad game. At the time of the holdout, he was crucial to the Dodgers' plans, as the team's only left-handed starter besides Osteen.

After the holdout, Johnny became expendable. In the 1966 season, he pitched only one and two-thirds innings in one game, an 8-5 loss to the Astros. It was April 19, 1966, and Podres relieved Don Drysdale in the fifth inning, allowing no runs and striking out a batter,

After 14 years, during which he provided the greatest moment in Dodgers history, it was his last time on the mound for the favorite team of his boyhood. On May 9, Bavasi traded him to the Detroit Tigers as part of a conditional deal (an undisclosed amount of cash and a player to be named later).

A new era dawned for the Dodgers. Only Gilliam, Koufax, Drysdale, and Roseboro remained from the Brooklyn club. Rookie Don Sutton (who made it to the Hall of Fame in 1998 after 324 career victories) replaced Podres in the rotation. The Dodgers won the National League pennant in 1966, but were swept by the Baltimore Orioles in the World Series. After the 1966 season, Sandy Koufax retired (and was elected to the Hall of Fame in his first year of eligibility in 1972), and Maury Wills was traded to Pittsburgh.

Beginning with the 1967 season, the team would decline precipitously. The Dodgers would not become competitive again until the early 1970s, led by a new generation of stars including Steve Garvey, Ron Cey, Davey Lopes, Bill Buckner, Crawford and Sutton.

Chapter Twelve
Life After L.A.

Johnny Podres' career spanned the most exciting years for the Brooklyn and Los Angeles Dodgers, 1953-1966. In those 14 seasons, the Dodgers won four world championships and six National League pennants. Johnny had compiled a 136-104 record, with a 3.68 earned-run average. His L.A. Dodger winning percentage of .562 (95-74), was even better than Drysdale's (.552, 187-152).

But it was over.

Bavasi gave Johnny a choice of four teams—Washington (managed by Hodges), Boston, Kansas City, or Detroit. Podres selected Detroit because he liked Manager Charlie Dressen, whom Johnny believed would give him a chance to pitch. Otherwise, Boston would have been his first choice, as it was closer to Witherbee. Bavasi kept Podres around as insurance during the Koufax/Drysdale hold-out. That hurt Podres' career because, once the holdout ended, Johnny didn't get a chance to pitch. Also, he spent over $1,000 fixing up his Los Angeles apartment after his marriage to Joan.

Bavasi stated that the trade would have been made even if Koufax and Drysdale did not sign, given the development of younger Dodger pitchers such as Sutton and Singer.

"I sent John to Detroit because Jim Campbell was the general manager and a close friend," Buzzie said recently. "And Jim promised that he would take care of John."

Like the Dodgers, the Tigers were pennant contenders, finishing fourth in 1965. The powerful offense included Al Kaline, Bill Freehan, Norm Cash, Willie Horton, and Dick McAuliffe. The pitching consisted of youngsters Denny McLain and Mickey Lolich, and veterans Dave Wickersham, Bill Monbouquette and Hank Aguirre. Detroit was seeking a seasoned "stopper" for its bullpen and Podres was to be used exclusively in relief.

"I just want to go somewhere where I can pitch," said Podres.

"I'm happy to be going with Charlie Dressen. I've been with him before, and he's one of the greatest managers I've ever played for."

One week after the trade, on May 16, Dressen suffered a heart attack. His successor, Bob Swift, caught for the Tigers when Bill Veeck's famous midget, Eddie Gaedel of the St. Louis Browns, walked in his only at-bat in 1951. After Swift took over as acting manager, the Tigers acquired pitcher Earl Wilson from the Red Sox, and Podres' opportunities dwindled. Then Swift became ill. He stepped down around the All-Star break, leaving the job to Frank Skaff. Swift died on October 17, 1966.

In Detroit, Podres was reunited with former Dodger teammates Larry Sherry, Don Demeter, and Dick Tracewski.

"When John came over," Sherry told us, "we hung pretty close together—so our teammates called us the Dodger guys, ex-National Leaguers, or sometimes worse! John was used in relief, though I think he started a few games. But most of the players didn't know him or ever saw him pitch in Brooklyn or L.A. They missed something great!"

On May 21, Detroit beat Baltimore, 3-2, and Podres picked up the save. His first American League victory came a few days later, when the Tigers beat the California Angels 5-4. John pitched one and one-third innings in relief of Wickersham and collected a single, before being lifted for Sherry. A two-run clout by McAuliffe proved to be decisive. On June 1, Podres won his second game (against one loss) with three and one-third scoreless innings in relief of Wickersham, as Detroit beat Minnesota, 9-4. Kaline drove in four runs for the Tigers. Six days later, he picked up another save in relief of Lolich and Sherry against the Red Sox, a 2-0 Detroit victory.

Podres and Sherry collaborated in pitching a scoreless inning against the Yankees on June 12, preserving McLain's ninth win, 7-5. McLain would win 20 games that year, and 31 in 1968. Continuing his mastery over the Yankees Podres (and Sherry) preserved Monbouquette's 4-3 victory on June 18. In the eighth, Podres retired Mantle on a line drive to shortstop Ray Oyler, got Maris on a pop fly, and struck out Pepitone. After retiring Elston Howard and Clete Boyer in the ninth, Johnny surrendered a double to Roy White and walked pinch-hitter Hector Lopez, causing Swift to bring in Sherry. Larry walked Jake Gibbs, but then retired Bobby Richardson to end the game.

Johnny Podres

On June 28, Podres finished out a win for Wilson against the Angels, as a recovering Dressen visited the clubhouse. In a rare start, the second game of a doubleheader against Cleveland on July 24, Johnny pitched six innings of one-run ball. Sherry picked up the victory as the Tigers won, 2-1. Two weeks later, he received another start, pitching eight innings of shutout ball against Washington. Sherry again relieved Podres, but gave up a two-run homer to Frank Howard. The game remained tied until the 12th, when Horton drove in two runs with a game-winning bases-loaded single. Two days later, Dressen died. Johnny was downcast, remembering Dressen as a great manager who taught him his famous change-up.

"That change-up he taught me in 1953 kept me going ever since," said Johnny.

Podres pitched eight innings without allowing an earned run on August 23 against Chicago, but did not get a decision. Sherry lost the game in the 12th, 2-1, on a sacrifice fly by Wayne Causey that scored Jerry Adair. Four days later, the Yankees finally got to Podres, pummeling him for seven runs in five and one-third innings, and beating Detroit 11-1. Then, on August 30, Johnny lost to the White Sox 3-1, giving up two runs in six innings. His season record stood at 2-4.

Johnny's first A.L. complete-game victory, a six-hit, 7-4 win over the Senators, came on September 5th. The Tigers scored on home runs by Cash, Kaline and Mickey Stanley. Two weeks later, he evened his record at four, with a brilliant, complete-game shutout against the Angels, 7-0. Podres held California to five hits and struck out five. He also led the Tigers' offensive attack, doubling in two runs.

Podres' record fell to 4-5 on October 2, his last appearance of the season. He gave up four earned runs in two and one-third innings, a 7-5 loss to Kansas City. For Detroit in '66, Johnny compiled a 3.43 ERA in 107 2/3 innings and saved four games. The Tigers finished the season in third place, 10 games behind Baltimore, with a record of 88-74.

Tigers in the Tank

"In 1967, Mayo Smith took over as manager with Johnny Sain as the pitching coach," Podres recalled. Sain acquired a near-legendary reputation for working with pitchers, but "Sain liked to work with the younger pitchers and didn't care much about the veterans."

The '67 Tigers featured most of the same personnel from '66, although Joe Sparma moved into the starting rotation and Mike Marshall, Pat Dobson, and John Hiller joined Podres and Sherry in the bullpen.

On June 4, Podres beat the Yanks, 11-7, for his first win, backed by a McAuliffe grand slam. Johnny threw three scoreless innings in relief of Aguirre, and Marshall finished the game. He won again on June 30, improving his record to 2-0 by beating Tommy John and the White Sox, 4-1. After seven and one-third innings without allowing a run, Podres was relieved by Marshall. Marshall gave up the Sox' only run on a single by Tommy Agee, but it was charged to Podres.

Exactly one month later, Johnny pitched seven innings of one-run ball, giving up only three hits (including Duane Josephson's first major league homer), while beating Chicago 7-1. Marshall pitched the final two innings and Horton led the Tiger offense with a three-run homer. It was Podres' third victory of the season, against no losses.

Mike Marshall, who had a fine rookie season for Detroit in 1967, went on to win the 1974 Cy Young Award as a member of the Dodgers. In '74, as the Dodgers advanced to the World Series for the first time since 1966, Marshall appeared in 106 games, winning 15 and saving 21, with a 2.42 earned-run average.

Marshall sat in the bullpen with Johnny many times during the '67 season.

"Although Podres was the highly-respected veteran and I was the wet-behind-the-ears rookie," Marshall told us, "it did not matter to him. Johnny embraces all in his presence and loves to have fun. At a team party with wives, he will get naked and jump into a teammate's pool."

Asked about this incident, Podres explained, "I won $1,400 on a $40 bet at the races and later that night went to a party at Joe Sparma's house. Somebody took the money out of my pocket and threw it in the pool. So I took off my clothes and dove in to retrieve my winnings."

On August 4, Podres suffered his first and only loss of the season (he finished with a 3-1 record and a 3.84 ERA, in 21 games). Duke Sims hit a three-run homer, and Johnny was tagged for two more runs in the first, as the Indians beat Detroit 11-5. Sam McDowell got the victory for Cleveland. Less than a week later, Podres was placed on the disabled list due to tendinitis in his left elbow. The Tigers called up Fred Lasher from Toledo to replace him.

Returning on September 10, Podres appeared in his last game for the Tigers, as Joel Horlen of the White Sox pitched a no-hitter against Detroit, winning 6-0. Podres pitched one and two-thirds scoreless innings in relief of Sparma.

The 1967 pennant race went down to the final week, even past the final game for the league-leading Red Sox (who had finished ninth the previous two seasons). Although Boston defeated Minnesota 5-2, creating

Johnny Podres

"pandemonium on the field," in the words of its broadcaster Ned Martin, the Sox still had to sweat out Detroit's doubleheader against the Angels, because a Tiger victory in the nightcap would force a one-game playoff. But California won 8-5, sealing the "Impossible Dream" season for the Red Sox. For the Tigers, blame focused on the bullpen, as four relievers (Hiller, Marshall, Wickersham, and Aguirre) let in five runs.

The Tigers finished 91-71, tied for second with Minnesota, one game behind the Red Sox. But they made up for it in 1968, winning the World Series in seven games against St. Louis. Sadly, Johnny Podres was no longer part of the Tiger plans. On October 19, Detroit released Podres and Jerry Lumpe, reportedly to make room for younger players.

Chapter Thirteen
Buzzie Comes Through

In 1968, Johnny Podres was out of major league baseball for the first time since 1952. He returned to Witherbee and "sold cars and vacuum cleaners to make a few bucks." One day, Johnny received a call from Buzzie Bavasi, asking if he could still pitch.

"I told him, 'Of course I can still pitch!' What else was I going to say? I wanted another shot."

Bavasi was part-owner of a new major league expansion franchise, the San Diego Padres. Johnny's near-namesake team would begin playing in the 1969 season.

On October 14-15, 1968, the Padres and the Montreal Expos in the National League and the Seattle Pilots and Kansas City Royals in the American League participated in the expansion draft. For the 1969 season, each league would be split into an "East" and "West" division consisting of six teams.

San Diego's first pick was Giants' outfielder Ollie Brown. It also selected Nate Colbert from Houston, Clarence (Cito) Gaston from Atlanta, Clay Kirby from St. Louis, Dick Selma from the Mets, and the Dodgers' Al Ferrara and Zoilo Versalles.

On November 5, the *New York Times* reported that Bavasi signed Podres to pitch in the instructional league in Phoenix "for the same $450 a month that the rookies get." Bavasi stated that Podres "could still pitch" and is "throwing good."

"We'll try him in spring training at Yuma," Bavasi said, "and he could be a once-a-week starter. It's certainly worth taking a chance, and he certainly wants to try it."

Bavasi stocked his staff with former Dodgers, including Preston Gomez as manager. Roger Craig became the pitching coach and Duke Snider the broadcaster. The hitting coach was Wally Moon, and one-time Dodger prospect Sparky Anderson also joined the coaching staff. He would lead the Cincinnati Reds to the pennant the following season.

On March 7, 1969, the Padres won their first spring training game when Podres shut out the Angels for the first three innings and got the victory, 11-5. The Padres signed Johnny to a major league contract on March 21. After pitching 12 and 2/3 scoreless innings in spring training, Johnny gave up his first runs that same day. Willie Mays hit a two-run homer in the third inning as the Giants and Juan Marichal beat San Diego, 9-6.

Al Ferrara suffered a broken ankle in 1968 and appeared in only two games. In 1967 he had his best year for the Dodgers, belting 16 home runs with an .812 OPS in 122 games. Those were pretty good numbers in the late 1960s, when pitchers reigned supreme. As Ferrara recalled,

"My era was real big on pitching, with Gibson, Marichal, Seaver, Jenkins and others. A dead ball era with high mounds and a long way to the fences."

Ferrara, Johnny's Dodger roommate from 1963-1966 also became Podres' new roommate with San Diego. He told us recently,

"John had not pitched in over a year. We hooked up again as members of the 1969 Padres. Bavasi was asked, why room those two together. 'Put them together,' he said, 'and you screw up one room, not two.'"

Manager Gomez told us how Johnny was such a valuable member of the team.

"He was like another pitching coach, helping all the younger pitchers. They all listened to him for advice. I really enjoyed being around Johnny as a pitcher and a human being. He is one of the best."

Podres' first start of the season, on April 9, proved he could still pitch effectively in the majors. In a 2-0 victory against the Astros, Johnny pitched seven scoreless innings of two-hit ball (allowing singles to Curt Blefary and Joe Morgan). Podres also knocked in one of San Diego's runs on a sacrifice fly. Tommie Sisk finished the shutout and Larry Dierker took the loss. Dierker recalled the situation for us.

"What I remember is that we were hoping to get a fast start in San Diego. Don Wilson pitched the opener and lost to a lesser pitcher in a low-scoring game. I knew Podres from growing up in Los Angeles. But I thought I would beat him as he was coming to the end of his career. He had great control that day and his famous 'pull the shade down' change-up."

On April 15, Podres returned to Dodger Stadium to face L.A. for the first time in his career. The Dodgers walloped San Diego, 14-0, for Johnny's first loss. Andy Kosco hit a grand slam off Podres in the fifth inning, breaking up a scoreless tie, and Johnny ended up yielding six runs in five innings before being lifted. Osteen pitched the shutout for the Dodgers. Here's what catcher Jeff Torborg remembered:

"A game which really stands out in my mind about Johnny was in 1969, when Buzzie Bavasi brought him to the San Diego Padres and he started against the Dodgers. He kept us so off balance with his change-up that he handcuffed us for about five innings. It looked like he was having the time of his life!"

Johnny lost again on April 21, to the Braves, 5-2. On May 2, he evened his record at 2-2, pitching four innings in relief of Clay Kirby, as Ferrara's grand slam lifted San Diego over the Reds, 8-5. Johnny picked up another relief win on May 10, as the Padres beat the Cardinals 5-3. In four and two-thirds innings in relief of Joe Niekro, Podres held St. Louis scoreless, yielding only one hit and striking out three. Roberto Pena's fourth inning grand slam was the deciding factor for the Padres.

Four days later, Ernie Banks hit a game-tying homer off Johnny in the bottom of the ninth, as the Padres lost to the Cubs, 3-2. Against Frank Reberger, in relief of Podres, pinch-hitter Willie Smith singled home former Dodger Nate Oliver for the victory, but Johnny suffered the loss, bringing his record to 3-3. But on May 25, Podres beat the Cubs, improving his record to 4-3. He pitched all nine innings and gave up only one earned run, as San Diego walloped Chicago 10-2, in the first game of a doubleheader. Colbert hit a grand slam for the Padres, and Ferrara and Brown also homered.

For the first time since 1952, on June 1, Johnny pitched in Montreal against the Expos. Before construction of Olympic Stadium in 1976, the Expos played in Jarry Park, a two-hour drive from Witherbee. Podres pitched seven innings of one-run ball (giving up a home run to Coco Laboy), as San Diego won 5-2, led by two Colbert home runs. John's record for the season stood at 5-3.

A week later, Johnny lost to the Mets at Shea Stadium in the second game of a doubleheader. Jerry Koosman got the victory, 4-1. The *New York Times* reported that Johnny was impressed by Koosman's pitching performance:

"He can really throw, and throw low," said Podres. Johnny also told Koosman,

"Keep the ball right here—at the knees—and you'll never get beat." In 1981, near the end of Koosman's career, Podres became his pitching coach with the Minnesota Twins.

Podres was effective against the Mets until the seventh, wiggling out of jams until he gave up a triple to Ron Swoboda that scored Cleon Jones.

On June 13, Podres' record fell to 5-5, with a loss to Philadelphia. Richie Allen and Mike Ryan homered off Johnny before he was lifted for Gary Ross, and the Phillies won 6-1. Against the Dodgers in Los Angeles on June 18, Podres lost again, bringing his record to 5-6. He failed to escape the third inning, giving up five runs, including a first-inning homer to Wes Parker. Sutton collected the 10-1 victory for the Dodgers, as future shortstop and manager Bill Russell played center field and collected two hits.

Johnny's last game was June 21, 1969 at Houston's Astrodome. He pitched one scoreless inning in relief of Dick Kelley, as the Astros defeated San Diego 4-0, the Padres' seventh loss in a row.

On June 27, Johnny retired and became the Padres' minor-league pitching instructor and a scout. According to Bavasi, "Everyone in the organization had to work two jobs." Johnny's place on the roster was taken by Walt Hriniak.

Ferrara, who hit .260 in 1969, with 14 homers and 56 RBIs, told us this about his boyhood idol who became his roommate:

"John was a big leaguer and he did things in a big league way, even for a team that was 30 games out in August. But the next thing I knew was that this guy who could still pitch in the big leagues was appointed the minor league pitching instructor for the Padres."

Coach Podres

"Bavasi made me the Padres' minor league pitching coach," Johnny said, "and from '69 to '73, I was a roving instructor in the organization in places like Salt Lake City, Alexandria, and Seattle. In 1973, I was hired as the major league pitching coach for Zim, who took over Gomez' job after the first 11 games of the 1972 season. Gomez went on to manage the Astros and the Cubs."

As pitching coach for the '73 Padres, Johnny worked with up-and-coming pitchers Randy Jones, Clay Kirby, Steve Arlin, Fred Norman and Mike Caldwell. Caldwell became one of Podres' special projects, developing into a fine major league pitcher. The Padres finished last in the National League West, with a record of 60-102.

Johnny Podres

Before he became an official major league pitching coach, Johnny had been helping his teammates for years. Former Dodger pitcher Pete Richert, now a high school pitching coach in the Palm Springs, California area, told us,

"He showed me how to use a change-up to be effective, and later as a pitching coach I used his knowledge to help in my own teaching."

Ken Rowe, who pitched briefly for the Dodgers in 1963, and has been active as a major and minor league pitching coach since 1975 (including 1985-1986 with the Baltimore Orioles), recalled that Johnny was always ready to teach his "great change-up, and above-average curve ball and fastball."

Danny McDevitt, a Brooklyn and Los Angeles Dodger pitcher from 1957-1960, is retired from the U.S. Department of Commerce and enjoys traveling with his son, a Delta pilot.

"Johnny had a nice fluid motion," McDevitt remembers, "and a good move to first base which he was kind enough to help me with since we were both left-handed. Johnny was such a good instructor, I think I picked off seven runners the first month."

Beginning with the 1974 season, Johnny joined the Boston Red Sox, spending five years as a minor league pitching instructor before making the parent club in 1980. Zimmer had become the Red Sox manager midway through the 1976 season.

The 1980 Red Sox boasted a number of quality pitchers in various phases of their careers, including Hall-of-Famer Dennis Eckersley, John Tudor, Mike Torrez, Dick Drago, Jack Billingham and Bill Campbell. Podres recalls working with youngsters Bob Ojeda and Bruce Hurst, both of whom went on to become successful major league pitchers. Johnny also recalls being Zimmer's personal "whipping boy."

"I used to hang out with Don after the games, sometimes at the racetrack, and he always blamed me when our pitchers gave up too many runs, or when we didn't win."

Evidently, Zimmer was on the hot seat. Although the Red Sox finished in fourth place, with an 83-77 record, Zimmer was fired with a few games remaining in the season. Sox icon Johnny Pesky took over, and Ralph Houk was hired for the strike-shortened 1981 season.

From 1981 through 1985, Johnny served as the pitching coach for the Minnesota Twins, working for manager Billy Gardner, while Zimmer moved on to the Texas Rangers. The Twins were cellar-dwellers when Podres joined the team, but rose to second-place in 1984, behind a strong staff that included Frank Viola, Mike Smithson, and John Butcher. But when Minnesota descended in the standings during the 1985 season, Gardner was fired, and Johnny left after the season.

In 1986, Johnny returned to the Dodgers as a minor league pitching coach, working with both Pedro and Ramon Martinez at the Dodgers' Las Palmas facility in the Dominican Republic.

As a pitching coach, Johnny believes that he made good pitchers better by instilling aggressiveness, confidence and a positive attitude. Johnny's techniques were "old school," eschewing charts and complex mechanics.

"I'd rather have my pitchers watch the game than keep a book on hitters," he told us.

He also enhanced his reputation as an expert on the change-up, successfully teaching the pitch to Viola, Ojeda, Tudor and Ramon Martinez.

The Last Championship Season

In 1990, Johnny began working with the Philadelphia Phillies. He became the major league pitching coach for manager Jim Fregosi in 1991, with a staff that included Curt Schilling, Andy Ashby and Mitch (Wild Thing) Williams.

"Johnny was the most positive pitching coach I have ever been around," Fregosi told us.

"He had a great ability to bring the best out of a person. He was great at teaching the change-up and the use of the lower body when making your turn towards home. Pitchers trusted Johnny's ability to help them and that he would always be there for them."

Fregosi also remembered that Podres wasn't too concerned with some of the game's modern methods, such as pitch counts.

"Whenever Johnny was counting pitches during a game, I would ask him how many pitches a certain pitcher had thrown. When a pitcher was throwing well, Johnny would count every other pitch. But when a pitcher was throwing poorly, I would hear him click that counter on every pitch."

The Phillies pitching staff featured the National League's worst earned-run average in 1992. Johnny remembered that the staff featured mostly "rejects"—pitchers who were past their prime, or developing pitchers who still had problems to work out, including Schilling, Danny Jackson, Terry Mulholland, and Tommy Greene. But in 1993, they led the league in complete games and captured the pennant.

In *More Than Beards, Bellies and Biceps: The Story of the 1993 Phillies* (Sports Publishing LLC, 2002), Johnny stated:

Johnny Podres

"Our starting pitching is what won it for us that year. Well, actually, it was three things. Our pitchers pitched like hell, our hitters hit like hell, and Fregosi managed like hell."

Curt Schilling, who owns racehorses that Johnny's son drives on the harness track in Saratoga, New York (a half-hour away from Johnny's home), considers Podres to be his greatest influence as a pitching coach:

"I give so much credit to Pods for my own success. Pods really built up my confidence that year and helped that pitching staff reach its potential. I was immature back in '93 but I grew up a lot that year, thanks to people like Johnny Podres. I was in awe of Pods, of what he had accomplished in his career."

Mitch Williams told us,

"Johnny helped me more than anybody because he talked very little about mechanics. He had a couple of little suggestions but mostly he dealt with the mental part of the game. Johnny is not a big man, but in his mind he was the biggest, baddest, S.O.B. on the field. And he was able to make his pitchers feel that way.

"I was pitching one day in a save situation, and I had just walked the bases loaded. Johnny came out, walked up to me and said,

'You're throwin' the ball fuckin' great.' I looked at him and said, 'are you watchin' the same shit I'm watchin'?' He said, 'Yeah they ain't hittin' you. Just throw it over.' He had a way of making you forget you were 'horseshit,' and I got out of it because he made me laugh. And it was like it was a new game. Johnny was the best pitching coach I ever had because he had an undying belief in you even when you sucked!! Thanks, Johnny, you made me better than I probably ever should have been!"

In the World Series, the Phillies lost to the Toronto Blue Jays when Williams gave up a memorable home run to Joe Carter.

"Williams had done a great job all season and Fregosi had to use him," Johnny told us, "even though both Mitch and Fregosi knew that he didn't have his best stuff."

After the '94 season, Johnny retired as the Phils' pitching coach, but continued to work with the Phillies until 1996, when he had the first of several heart bypass operations.

Chapter Fourteen
Time for Reflection

At the age of 64, time and toil on the mound conspired to make a retiree of the young pitcher and the old coach. "Use it or lose it" may be wisdom, but overuse can lead to loss as well. For a pitcher, there may be debilitation of the shoulder and arm. The training table with its thick steaks can clog arteries. The full-windup drive off the pitching rubber can wear out the hips and knees.

For Podres, the shoulder and arm survived all the stress, but the hip and knee joints did not. Of course, there was also the chronic bad back. Climbing out of a dugout and walking to a mound to counsel a pitcher while a reliever warms up was over.

At age 72, he moves deftly around the house and yard and walks his dog, Andre, in the neighborhood but takes no more hikes along Adirondack mountain trout streams. He fishes from boats on ponds and lakes. Deer hunting in the North Country is a memory. Many baseball fans remember him and his daily mail includes letters from admirers.

"I take 10 pills a day now. I've had six bypasses and a couple of stents. I was thinking about hip replacement but the doctor said it's risky, and they might leave me on the operating table." Instead, he works out regularly in a swimming pool.

Driving his car is no problem. Recently he cruised down the Adirondack Northway and the New York Thruway to baseball memorabilia events in New York and New Jersey as the 50th anniversary of his Brooklyn World Series victories of 1955 approached. He signed hundreds of autographs and had a good time, reuniting with Don Newcombe, Willie Mays, Maury

Wills and Don Larsen, among others. Johnny Podres complains about aches and pains, but he still gets around and attended spring training and fantasy camps over the eight years after his retirement as a pitching coach.

Walking seems to be no problem for some elderly shoppers as they traverse a mall. Likewise motivated, Podres seems to have no trouble when he wants to make his way to a horse track betting window or clubhouse. Johnny Podres gets around.

Mostly, however, he's a homebody and he likes it. He's comfortable in athletic shoes, blue jeans and knit shirts, favorite attire all his life. If you spend a morning with him at home in upstate New York, the phone will ring time and again. Today the first to call is former roomie Al Ferrara, who wants to know what Johnny thinks about a horse running later that day in southern California, but mostly just wants to chat with an old buddy.

Next is Don Zimmer, who asks if Johnny wants to put some dough on a horse in Florida. This day Zimmer tells Johnny he'll be at a track before he attends a party in the evening. More than half a century after Zim introduced Pod to horse racing, they are still at it together.

"Zimmer said he called Buzzie (Bavasi) last night and wished him a happy birthday. It was his 90th. He asked Buzzie what he thought about guys getting $50 million contracts these days when Buzzie gave him only $25,000 for managing a whole team (the Padres). Buzzie told him he was overpaid."

When he hung up he reminded us that he and Zim were roommates on the Dodgers for five years. When Los Angeles traded Zimmer to the Cubs Johnny made him a promise.

"I told him if I was ever pitching against the Cubs in a game where we were way ahead and he came up to bat I'd throw him a fat one."

That promise was well documented by Zimmer in his autobiography, but the details are in dispute. The Dodgers were ahead 9-1 late in the game. Zimmer says Johnny tossed him a wicked curve and an outside corner fastball, wasted one and then fired what catcher John Roseboro said was probably the only spitball Podres ever threw. Zimmer swung in self defense and missed.

"That's horseshit," Johnny told us. "The first two strikes were fastballs right down the middle. Once a .235 hitter, always a .235 hitter."

The two of them still needle each other as they compare horses with their racing forms in the morning, but nobody calls Johnny in the afternoon. That's when he's intent on placing bets at tracks all over the country through New York Off-Track Betting. Then he turns on the racing channel to see how his horses make out.

Johnny Podres

"I might only bet five or six bucks in a day, but I've had days where I won $500," he told us.

"About three o'clock I'll have a glass of Merlot when Joanie starts preparing dinner. You know, she's just a wonderful woman -- and she still gives figure skating lessons. Then I'll have another when I sit down with her, but it's only for medicinal purposes you understand. I used to drink a lot after a game when I was single, but I never liked beer much. I liked something sweeter. The clubhouse boy always had a lot of beer ready for everybody else, but he had a V.O. and Seven for me. He even used to put a carton of cigarettes in your locker."

At 6 o'clock or so he turns in, but really only naps for a couple of hours, because he gets up and watches television late into the night. He likes some news talk shows and documentaries and, of course, some baseball games. The playoffs and World Series of '04 captured his attention. The Red Sox won more than the Series but also, as a team, the same honor Podres won as an individual 49 years earlier.

"Yeah, they deserved to be Sportsmen of the Year because they played so well together as a team when it counted. "

Not likely to win that award any time soon are ballplayers on steroids.

"Steroids are really all their own problems -- it's their health that's mostly at risk."

Should the pitchers be upset that steroid-pumped sluggers might ruin their records?

"Hell, they might be on them, too, for all I know."

Johnny's two sons both played baseball in high school, but never went further in the sport. One developed shoulder trouble and the other had eyesight problems (long since corrected with laser surgery). Johnny likes Little League and other organized sports programs for kids but is appalled that some coaches, bent on victory, don't want to let every kid play.

"You've got to give all the kids a chance to play and enjoy it at that stage in life."

Looking back, he attributes a lot of his success to the changeup that Charlie Dressen taught him, and he picked up a baseball to show us how he threw it.

"Charlie said to pretend that your index and middle fingers are cut off to stubs," he said as he split the two digits to a "V" and lifted them away from the ball. That slowed it down a lot from the 92-93 miles per hour fastball I had. It was a one-speed change from the fastball, which was faster or slower on some days."

Afterword

Johnny Podres provided the greatest thrill Brooklyn Dodgers fans ever experienced, won their adulation and easily could have been elected president of the borough 50 years ago. Everywhere he went in Brooklyn he was greeted with cheers and awe and reverence.

Continuing a long career as a pitcher and coach, he crossed paths with a lot of ballplayers, both teammates and opponents. We talked to many of them and researched the opinions of many others. They all, without exception, had nothing but good things to say about the boy and the man, about the way he conducted himself on and off the field.

One of those who said it best is Roger Craig, a teammate on the Brooklyn Dodgers, an outstanding pitcher who went on to be a major league manager. He won Game Five of the '55 Series. He still has his '55 World Series ring and said winning that Series was one of the happiest moments of his life. When Johnny won the Corvette as Most Valuable Player, he let Craig drive it once in awhile.

"Johnny was a fierce competitor with a great arm, a great fastball and one of the best straight change-ups I ever saw. He was a big-game pitcher with great mechanics. He didn't pace himself. He gave everything he had. Sometimes he got tired and usually was honest with Alston and told him to get somebody else ready.

"Johnny was a free spirit. He was a fun-loving guy. He liked to have a few cocktails. He had a great knowledge of the game and was a great student of the game and a great teammate. He could have been a good manager in the majors if he wanted to."

Today, Brooklyn's all-time biggest sports hero, the only Brooklyn Dodger to kill the Yankees and win the World Series, the player who did more for the borough than any other, remains true to his upstate small town roots. Nobody ever accused him of trying to be the big shot he really is in the minds of old-time Dodgers fans. We first interviewed him in the early '60s, when he was in his prime pitching for Los Angeles. He was gracious and generous with his time. Just as he was then, despite all of his accomplishments, Johnny Podres is a regular guy.

"Hey," he says, "you've just got to be who you are."

Appendix
Johnny Podres' Statistics

John Joseph Podres
b. September 30, 1932, Witherbee, New York, U.S.A.
Batted left, threw left.
Height 5'11"
Weight 192 lbs.

Pitching

Year	Ag	Tm	Lg	W	L	G	GS	GF	CG	SHO	SV	IP	H	R	ER	HR	BB	SO	HBP	WP	ERA
1953	20	BRO	NL	9	4	33	18	3	3	1	0	115.0	126	62	54	12	64	82	1	2	4.23
1954	21	BRO	NL	11	7	29	21	4	6	2	0	151.7	147	77	72	13	53	79	1	3	4.27
1955	22	BRO	NL	9	10	27	24	0	5	2	0	159.3	160	80	70	15	57	114	4	5	3.95
1957	24	BRO	NL	12	9	31	27	4	10	6	3	196.0	168	64	58	15	44	109	1	3	2.66
1958	25	LA	NL	13	15	39	31	4	10	2	1	210.3	208	96	87	27	78	143	2	4	3.72
1959	26	LA	NL	14	9	34	29	1	6	2	0	195.0	192	93	89	23	74	145	3	8	4.11
1960	27	LA	NL	14	12	34	33	1	8	1	0	227.7	217	88	78	25	71	159	1	7	3.08
1961	28	LA	NL	18	5	32	29	2	6	1	0	182.7	192	81	76	27	51	124	4	8	3.74
1962	29	LA	NL	15	13	40	40	0	8	0	0	255.0	270	121	108	20	71	178	3	4	3.81
1963	30	LA	NL	14	12	37	34	3	10	5	1	198.3	196	91	78	16	64	134	3	5	3.54
1964	31	LA	NL	0	2	2	2	0	0	0	0	2.7	5	5	5	1	3	0	0	1	16.88
1965	32	LA	NL	7	6	27	22	4	2	1	1	134.0	126	57	51	17	39	63	2	6	3.43
1966	33	LA	NL	0	0	1	0	0	0	0	0	1.7	2	0	0	0	1	1	0	0	0.00
		DET	AL	4	5	36	13	12	2	1	4	107.7	106	48	41	12	34	53	1	4	3.43
		TOT		4	5	37	13	12	2	1	4	109.3	108	48	41	12	35	54	1	4	3.38
1967	34	DET	AL	3	1	21	8	6	0	0	1	63.3	58	29	27	12	11	34	1	3	3.84
1969	36	SD	NL	5	6	17	9	2	1	0	0	64.7	66	34	31	7	28	17	1	3	4.31
15 Yr WL%			.561	148	116	440	340	46	77	24	11	2265.0	2239	1026	925	242	743	1435	28	66	3.68

Hitting

Year	Ag	Tm	Lg	G	AB	R	H	2B	3B	HR	RBI	SB	CS	BB	SO	BA	OBP	SLG	TB	SH	SF	IBB	HBP	GDP
1953	20	BRO	NL	34	36	5	11	0	0	0	1	1	0	0	1	.306	.324	.306	11	1	0	0	1	1
1954	21	BRO	NL	38	60	7	17	3	1	0	4	0	0	5	5	.283	.328	.367	22	3	2	0	0	2
1955	22	BRO	NL	32	60	9	11	2	0	0	5	0	1	4	5	.183	.234	.217	13	4	0	0	0	1
1957	24	BRO	NL	35	72	6	15	4	0	0	4	0	1	2	5	.208	.230	.264	19	3	0	0	0	2
1958	25	LA	NL	42	71	5	9	0	0	0	4	0	0	2	17	.127	.147	.127	9	4	2	0	0	0
1959	26	LA	NL	34	65	4	16	1	0	0	4	0	0	6	13	.246	.306	.262	17	3	1	0	0	1
1960	27	LA	NL	34	66	3	9	0	0	0	3	0	0	5	15	.136	.205	.136	9	10	1	0	1	0
1961	28	LA	NL	32	69	3	16	2	0	0	7	0	0	2	8	.232	.250	.261	18	4	1	0	0	2
1962	29	LA	NL	40	88	6	14	2	0	1	5	0	0	2	8	.159	.187	.216	19	5	0	0	1	1
1963	30	LA	NL	37	64	6	9	2	0	1	8	0	0	1	11	.141	.147	.219	14	3	3	0	0	0
1964	31	LA	NL	2	0	0	0	0	0	0	0	0	0	0	0		1.000		0	0	0	0	1	0
1965	32	LA	NL	27	45	1	8	0	0	0	2	0	0	1	8	.178	.196	.178	8	1	0	0	0	0
1966	33	DET	AL	36	30	5	7	3	0	0	2	0	0	2	5	.233	.281	.333	10	0	0	0	0	2
		TOT		37	30	5	7	3	0	0	2	0	0	2	5	.233	.281	.333	10	0	0	0	0	2
1967	34	DET	AL	21	20	1	2	0	0	0	0	0	0	0	4	.100	.100	.100	2	0	0	0	0	2
1969	36	SD	NL	17	16	0	1	0	0	0	1	0	0	0	3	.062	.059	.062	1	2	0	0	0	0
				462	762	61	145	19	1	2	50	1	2	32	108	.190	.224	.226	172	43	11	0	4	14

147

Fielding

Year	Ag	Tm	Lg	Pos	G	PO	A	E	DP	FP
1953	20	BRO	NL	P	33	6	17	1	0	.958
1954	21	BRO	NL	P	29	11	15	1	0	.963
1955	22	BRO	NL	P	27	7	21	1	2	.966
1957	24	BRO	NL	P	31	9	32	1	3	.976
1958	25	LA	NL	P	39	7	25	2	3	.941
1959	26	LA	NL	P	34	6	37	2	5	.956
1960	27	LA	NL	P	34	8	30	1	4	.974
1961	28	LA	NL	P	32	6	26	1	2	.970
1962	29	LA	NL	P	40	4	31	6	1	.854
1963	30	LA	NL	P	37	2	33	0	1	1.000
1964	31	LA	NL	P	2	0	0	0	0	
1965	32	LA	NL	P	27	3	15	1	1	.947
1966	33	LA	NL	P	1	0	1	0	0	1.000
		DET	AL	P	36	7	14	1	1	.955
		TOT		P	37	7	15	1	1	.957
1967	34	DET	AL	P	21	3	7	0	1	1.000
1969	36	SD	NL	P	17	1	9	0	0	1.000
					440	80	313	18	24	.956

148

Postseason Pitching

Year	Tm	Opp	G	GS	ERA	W-L	SV	CG	SHO	IP	H	ER	BB	SO
1953	BRO	NY	1	1	3.38	0-1	0	0	0	2.7	1	1	2	0
1955	BRO	NY	2	2	1.00	2-0	0	2	1	18.0	15	2	4	10
1959	LA	CH	2	2	4.82	1-0	0	0	0	9.3	7	5	6	4
1963	LA	NY	1	1	1.08	1-0	0	0	0	8.3	6	1	1	4
			6	6	2.11	4-1	0	2	1	38.3	29	9	13	18

Postseason Hitting

Year	Round	Tm	Opp	G	AB	R	H	2B	3B	HR	RBI	BB	SO	BA	OBP	SLG	SB	CS	SH	SF	HBP
1953	WS	BRO	NY	1	1	0	1	0	0	0	0	0	0	1.000	1.000	1.000	0	0	0	0	0
1955	WS	BRO	NY	2	7	1	1	0	0	0	0	0	1	.143	.143	.143	0	0	1	0	0
1959	WS	LA	CH	3	4	1	2	1	0	0	1	0	0	.500	.500	.750	0	0	0	0	0
1963	WS	LA	NY	1	4	0	1	0	0	0	0	0	0	.250	.250	.250	0	0	0	0	0
				7	16	2	5	1	0	0	1	0	1	.312	.312	.375	0	0	1	0	0

Record Against the New York Yankees

Year	Tm	G	GS	ERA	W-L	SV	CG	SHO	IP	H	ER	BB	SO
1953	BRO	1	1	3.38	0-1	0	0	0	2.7	1	1	2	0
1955	BRO	2	2	1.00	2-0	0	2	1	18.0	15	2	4	10
1963	LA	1	1	1.08	1-0	0	0	0	8.3	6	1	1	4
1966	DET	5	1	6.94	0-1	0	0	0	11.7	20	9	5	4
1967	DET	1	0	0.00	1-0	0	0	0	3.0	1	0	1	1
TOTAL:		10	5	2.68	4-2	0	2	1	43.7	43	13	13	19

All-Star: 1958, 1960, 1962
Awards: 1955 WS MVP

Leaders:

ERA
1957-2.66-1
1960-3.08-8

Wins
1958-13-9
1961-18-4

Winning Percentage
1953 .692 - 7
1959 .609 - 8
1961 .783 - 1

Strikeouts Per Nine Innings
1955-6.44-3
1957-5.01-9
1958-6.12-4
1959-6.69-3
1960-6.29-8
1961-6.11-9
1962-6.28-8

Innings Pitched
1958-210.3-10
1962-255.0-10

Strikeouts
1955-114-8
1958-143-3
1959-145-7
1960-159-8
1962-178-6

Games Started
1958-31-9
1960-33-9
1962-40-2
1963-34-9

Shutouts
1955-2-7
1957-6-1
1958-2-6
1963-5-5

Dodgers All-Time Rankings:

Games Pitched
Don Sutton	550
Don Drysdale	518
Jim Brewer	474
Ron Perranoski	457
Clem Labine	425
Charlie Hough	401
Sandy Koufax	397
Brickyard Kennedy	381
Dazzy Vance	378
Johnny Podres	366

Games Started
Don Sutton	533
Don Drysdale	465
Claude Osteen	335
Brickyard Kennedy	332
Dazzy Vance	326
F. Valenzuela	320
Sandy Koufax	314
Johnny Podres	310
Orel Hershiser	303
Burleigh Grimes	285

Games Won
Don Sutton	233
Don Drysdale	209
Dazzy Vance	190
Brickyard Kennedy	174
Sandy Koufax	165
Burleigh Grimes	158
Claude Osteen	147
F. Valenzuela	141
Johnny Podres	136
Nap Rucker	134

Games Lost
Don Sutton	181
Don Drysdale	166
Brickyard Kennedy	150
Nap Rucker	134
Dazzy Vance	131
Claude Osteen	126
Burleigh Grimes	121
F. Valenzuela	116
Johnny Podres	104
Orel Hershiser	102

Strikeouts
Don Sutton	2696
Don Drysdale	2486
Sandy Koufax	2396
Dazzy Vance	1918
F. Valenzuela	1759
O. Hershiser	1443
Johnny Podres	1331
Ramon Martinez	1314
Bob Welch	1292
Nap Rucker	1217

Shutouts
Don Sutton	52
Don Drysdale	49
Sandy Koufax	40
Nap Rucker	38
Claude Osteen	34
Dazzy Vance	30
F. Valenzuela	29
Jeff Pfeffer	25
O. Hershiser	24
Johnny Podres	23
Bob Welch	23

Dodgers World Series Leaders:

Games Pitched
Carl Erskine	11
Clem Labine	10
Hugh Casey	9
Sandy Koufax	8
Don Drysdale	7
Johnny Podres	6
Joe Hatten	6
Burt Hooton	6
Don Sutton	6
Several tied at	5

Innings Pitched
Sandy Koufax	57
Carl Erskine	42
Don Sutton	41
Don Drysdale	40
Orel Hershiser	40
Johnny Podres	38
Burt Hooton	32
Clem Labine	27
Don Newcombe	22
Claude Osteen	21

Won-Loss Record
Johnny Podres	4-1
Sandy Koufax	4-3
Don Drysdale	3-3
Burt Hooton	3-3
Orel Hershiser	2-0
Larry Sherry	2-0
Tommy John	2-1
Preacher Roe	2-1
Hugh Casey	2-2
Carl Erskine	2-2
Clem Labine	2-2
Don Sutton	2-2

Strikeouts
Sandy Koufax	61
Don Drysdale	36
Carl Erskine	31
Don Sutton	26
Burt Hooton	24
Don Newcombe	19
Johnny Podres	18
Orel Hershiser	17
Clem Labine	13
Tommy John	13

Shutouts
Sandy Koufax	2
Johnny Podres	1
Burleigh Grimes	1
Preacher Roe	1
Clem Labine	1
Don Drysdale	1
Claude Osteen	1
Orel Hershiser	1

Earned Run Average (minimum 18 innings)
Claude Osteen	0.86
Sherry Smith	0.89
Sandy Koufax	0.95
Orel Hershiser	1.09
Clem Labine	1.65
Johnny Podres	2.12
Preacher Roe	2.54
Joe Black	2.54
Don Drysdale	2.95
Burt Hooton	3.74

Index

A

Aaron, Hank, 8
Adair, Jerry, 127
Adirondack Mountains, 15
Aguirre, Hank, 126
Ali, Muhammed, 59
Allen, Richie, 118, 134
Allen, Steve, 56
Allison, Bob, 122
Alou, Felipe, 87, 96–97, 114
Alou, Jesus, 119
Alou, Matty, 97
Alston, Walter, 9, 11, 23, 26, 28, 28–29, 40, 42–45, 53, 64–65, 72–80, 84–85, 87–88, 93, 97–98, 111–112, 114–115, 117–121, 143
Amoros, Sandy, 6, 28, 44–45, 48–49, 53, 64, 81
Anderson, Clary, 18
Anderson, Sparky, 71, 132
Anderson, Wayne, 85
Aparicio, Luis, 74–75
Arizona Diamondbacks, 117
Arlin, Steve, 134
Ashburn, Richie, 94
Ashby, Andy, 136
Aspromonte, Bob, 91, 114

B

Bailey, Ed, 97
Bainbridge Naval Training Station, 61
Baker, Naomi, 52
Baltimore Memorial Stadium, 71
Bankhead, Tallulah, 115
Banks, Ernie, 65, 133
Bannister, Roger, 5, 35, 59
Barber, Red, 15
Battey, Earl, 75, 122
Bauer, Hank, 22
Bavasi, Buzzie, ix, xii, 23, 25, 35, 52, 62, 83–84, 88, 91, 111, 118, 122–123, 125, 131–134, 140
Becker, Joe, 11, 52, 84
Beckert, Glenn, 119
Belmont Park, 26
Bennett, Dennis, 9
Berra, Yogi, ix, 22, 44, 48–49, 52–53, 80

Bessent, Don, 36, 62
Bilko, Steve, 71
Billingham, Jack, 135
Black, Joe, 4, 153
Blefary, Curt, 132
Boone, Ray, 75
Bossert Hotel, 34, 55–56
Boston Red Sox, 17, 59, 135
Bouton, Jim, 13
Boyer, Clete, 10, 12, 126
Boyer, Ken, 64, 115
"Boys of Summer," 2, 21, 27, 163
Branca, Ralph, 3
Braves, Milwaukee, 29, 64, 72, 85
Breeding, Marv, 113
Brewer, Jim, 117, 152
Bright, Harry, 7
Broglio, Ernie, 95, 115
Brosnan, Jim, 23
Brown, Ollie, 131
Buckner, Bill, 123
Bums, 2–3, 5, 51, 55, 94
Burlington Cardinals, 18
Burlington, Vermont, 18–19, 87
Burright, Larry, ix, 24, 97
Butcher, John, 135
Butinski, Benny, 16
Byrne, Tommy, 43, 52, 62

C

Caldwell, Mike, 134
Callison, Johnny, 75
Camilli, Dolf, 96
Camilli, Doug, 96
Campanella, Roy 4–5, 21, 24, 41–45, 48–49, 66, 69, 72, 78
Campbell, Bill, 135
Campbell, Jim, xii, 125
Caray, Harry, 115
Carter, Joe, 137
Cash, Norm, 75, 125

Causey, Wayne, 127
Cepeda, Orlando, 87, 96–97
Cerv, Bob, 41–42
Cey, Ron, 123
Chambliss, Chris, 22
Chavez Ravine, 68, 70, 94
Chicago Cubs, 112, 120
Chicago White Sox, 74–77, 127–128
Churn, Chuck, ix, 74
Cimoli, Gino, 66, 71
Cincinnati Reds, 8, 132
Clay, Cassius, 55
Colbert, Nate, 131, 133
Cole, Nat King, 68, 72
Coliseum, Los Angeles Memorial 70
Collins, Joe, 22
Comiskey Park, 75, 78
Coney Island, 17
Conine, Jeff, 22
Conley, Gene, 64
Connors, Chuck, 68
Cox, Billy, 21
Craig, Roger, ix, 40, 53, 64, 71–73, 75, 77–78, 81, 86, 88, 91, 113, 132, 143
Crawford, Willie, 14, 117, 123
Crosley Field, 64
Cuccinello, Tony, 76

D

Daffiness Boys, 2
Daley, Arthur, 122
Dangerfield, Rodney, 2, 56
Daniel Freeman Hospital, 116, 122
Dark, Alvin, 96
Davenport, Thomas, 15
Davidson, Matt, 17
Davis, Sammy Jr., 68

Davis, Tommy 8, 10–11, 13, 81, 96–98, 121
Davis, Willie, 9–10, 12–13, 81, 84, 87–88, 91, 96, 115, 117, 119–120
Demeter, Don, ix, 62, 73, 77, 80, 86, 126
Desmond, Connie, 15
Detroit Tigers, 71, 79, 103, 123
Dierker, Larry, ix, 113, 132
DiMaggio, Joe, 11, 40
Dobson, Pat, 127
Doby, Larry, 75
Donatelli, Augie, 120
Donovan, Dick, 77, 79
Downing, Al, ix, 7–10, 12, 14
Drago, Dick, 135
Dressen, Charlie, 3, 22–23, 26, 28, 79, 103, 125–127, 141
Drysdale, Don, xi–xii, 6, 8–9, 12–13, 23, 25, 36, 62, 66, 69, 71, 73, 77–78, 80, 83, 85, 88, 91–97, 101, 112, 114–117, 119–123, 125, 152–153
Durocher, Leo, 7, 28, 84–85, 97, 111–112, 118
Durslag, Melvin, 85
Dwyer, William, 17, 57

E

Ebbets Field, 1, 3, 17–18, 33, 40–42, 51, 63–64, 67, 163
Eckersley, Dennis 13, 135
Edwards, Johnny, 113
Ennis, Del, 64, 75
Erskine, Carl, 3–5, 22–23, 25, 32, 36, 40, 54, 62, 153
Essegian, Chuck, ix, 76

F

Fairly, Ron, 8, 14, 71, 85, 88, 96–97, 112, 115, 118, 122
Farrell, Dick, 86–88, 91
Fenway Park, 3
Ferrara, Al, ix, 6, 114–115, 118, 131–134, 140
Finch, Frank, 121
Flood, Curt, 122
Flushing Meadows, 67
Ford, Whitey, 7–8, 13, 42
Fowler, Art, 71
Fox, Nellie, 74–75
Freehan, Bill, 125
Freese, Gene, 87, 119
Fregosi, Jim, ix, 136–137
Frisch, Frank, 52
Furillo, Carl, 4, 15, 21, 28, 48, 64, 66, 71, 73, 77, 81

G

Gabrielson, Len, 119
Gaedel, Eddie, 126
Gallego, Mike, 22
Gardner, Billy, 135
Garvey, Steve, 123
Gaston, Clarence, 131
Gehrig, Lou, 39
Gentile, Jim, 69
Gibbs, Jake, 126
Gibson, Bob, 115
Gibson, Kirk, 13
Gilliam, Jim, 9, 11, 13–14, 21, 28, 43–45, 48, 53, 73, 75–76, 78–79, 91, 98, 118, 121, 123
Gionfriddo, Al, 11
Gleason, Jackie, 2
Glebus, Anthony, 54
Goldberg, Molly, 2
Golden, Jim, 71, 91

Gomez, Preston, ix, 118, 132, 134
Goodman, Billy, 76
Grant, Jim, 121
Gray, Dick, ix, 70
Greene, Tommy, 136
Groat, Dick, 115

H

Harkness, Tim, 87
Harper, Tommy, 113
Harriman, Averill, 58
Harris, Gail, 81
Hazard, Kentucky, xi, 19
Hendley, Bob, 120
Herman, Billy, 54
Hershiser, Orel, 59, 152–153
Hiller, John, 127, 129
Hoak, Don, 43
Hodges, Gil, 5, 15, 21–22, 34, 42, 44–45, 48–49, 53, 56, 64, 66, 68, 71, 73, 77, 81, 83, 91, 112, 125
Hodges, Joan, ix, 56
Hollywood Park, 68, 85
Horton, Willie, 125, 127–128
Houk, Ralph, 8, 135
Houston Colt 45s, 91, 95
Howard, Elston, 10–11, 14, 45, 48, 126
Howard, Frank, 8, 10, 13–14, 71, 81, 87–88, 94–97, 112–113, 115, 117, 121, 127
Howell, Dixie 40
Hriniak, Walt, 134
Hughes, Jim, 22
Hunt, Ron, 113
Hunter, Bob, 83
Hunter, Willard, 91
Hurst, Bruce, 135

I

Isabel, Alex, 17

J

Jackson, Danny, 136
Jarry Park, 133
Jersey City, 65
John, Tommy, 128, 153
Johnny Podres Field, 57
Johnson, Darrell, 87
Johnson, Lou, 121
Jones, Cleon, 134
Jones, Mack, 118
Jones, Randy, 104, 134
Jordan, Michael, 59
Josephson, Duane, 128

K

Kaline, Al, 125–127
Kanehl, Rod, 94
Kansas City Royals, 131
Karros, Eric, 22
Kasko, Eddie, 94
Kazlo, Steve, 17, 57
Kelley, Dick, 134
Kennedy, John, 117
Kerlan, Dr. Robert, xi, 83, 85, 112, 116, 118
Killebrew, Harmon, 122
Kirby, Clay, 104, 131, 133–134
Klippstein, Johnny, 71
Kluszewski, Ted, 22, 64, 75
Koosman, Jerry, 133
Kosco, Andy, 133
Koufax, Sandy, xi–xii, 6–8, 10, 12–13, 23, 24–25, 32, 59, 63, 69, 71–72, 74, 78, 81, 84–85, 88, 91–97, 100–101, 112–113, 115, 117, 119–123, 125, 152–153

Kubek, Tony, 7, 9–10, 62
Kuenn, Harvey 96–97

L

Labine, Clem, ix, 4–5, 22, 25, 36, 43, 56, 64–65, 68–71, 74–75, 78, 81, 91, 152–153
Laboy, Coco, 133
Lake Champlain, 15, 18
Landis, Jim, ix, 75, 78–79
Larker, Norm, ix, 73, 75, 77–78, 81, 91
Larsen, Don, 62, 96, 140
Lasher, Fred, 128
Lefebvre, Jim, 115, 121
LeRoy, Mervyn, 94
Linney Athletic Field, 57
Loes, Billy, 4, 25
Logan, Johnny, 24
Lolich, Mickey, 126
Lollar, Sherm, 74–79
Lopes, Davey, 123
Lopez, Al, 74
Lopez, Hector, ix, 11, 126
Los Angeles Times, 8–9, 11–12, 17, 23, 86–87, 95, 111, 114, 116, 118, 121
Lown, Turk, 74
Lumpe, Jerry, 129

M

Maglie, Sal, 36, 64
Mantilla, Felix, 73, 94
Mantle, Mickey, 7–8, 10–14, 22, 24, 28, 43, 48, 54, 57, 80, 100, 126
Marciano, Rocky, 46
Marichal, Juan, 87, 96–97, 119, 132
Maris, Roger, 7–11, 14, 126

Marshall, Mike, ix, 127–129
Martin, Billy, 43–44
Martin, Dean, 68
Martin, J.C., 75
Martinez, Pedro, 94
Martinez, Ramon, 136, 152
Mary Fletcher Hospital, 87
Massie's Restaurant, 68
Maxvill, Dal, 95
Mays, Willie, 28, 63, 87, 96–97, 114, 121, 132, 139
Mazeroski, Bill, 8
McAuliffe, Dick, 125–126, 128
McCarver, Tim, 115
McCovey, Willie, 96
McDaniel, Lindy, 72
McDevitt, Danny, ix, 64, 72, 74, 135
McDougald, Gil, ix, 28, 43–45
McLain, Denny, 126
McMillan, Roy, 119
McMullen, Ken, ix, 92
Meyer, Russ, 4, 22, 42, 54
Mickens, Glenn, ix, 22–23
Miller, Bob, 113–114, 117–119, 121
Miller, Larry, 117
Miller, Stu, 96
Mincher, Don, 121
Mineville, New York, 15–17, 57
Minnesota Twins, 104, 121, 134–135
Moeller, Joe, 116–117
Monbouquette, Bill, 126
Montreal Royals, 18, 21, 31
Moon, Wally, ix, 68, 71, 73, 76–77, 79, 81, 83–84, 87–88, 121, 132
Moore, Ray, 80
Morgan, Joe, 132
Moriah, New York, 16, 57

Moses, Robert, 67
Mountain State League, 19
Mulholland, Terry, 136
Mulleavy, Greg, 118
Mullin, Willard, 2
Murray, Jim, 12, 23, 86, 114
Musial, Stan, 2, 9, 35, 64, 86, 115
Myers, Kenny, 9

N

Neal, Charlie, 66, 71, 73, 75–79, 88, 91
Nen, Dick, 115, 117
Newcombe, Don, xi, 3, 5, 21–23, 25, 35, 40, 52, 64, 66, 71, 87, 139, 153
Newport News, Virginia, 19
New York Giants, 4–5, 28, 40, 49, 65, 68, 72, 87, 94, 96, 112, 131
New York Mets, 18, 23, 68–69, 91, 94, 96, 99, 112–113, 116, 119, 131, 133–134
New York *Times*, 12, 122, 131, 133
Niekro, Joe, 133
Norfolk Naval Base, 61
Norman, Fred, 104, 134
Northern League, 18

O

O'Dell, Billy, 95–96
Ojeda, Bob, 135
Oliver, Gene, 95
Oliver, Nate, 133
Olympic Stadium, 133
O'Malley, Kay, 94
O'Malley, Walter, xii, 23, 29, 34, 52, 66–68, 70, 94, 111–112, 122

Ortega, Phil, 117
Osteen, Claude, ix, xii, 117, 121–122, 133, 152–153
Oyler, Ray, 126
Ozark, Danny, 118

P

Pagan, Jose, 97, 114
Palmer, Arnold, 59
Parker, Wes, 117, 119, 121–122, 134
Pearson, Albie, 116
Pedroza, Alma, 94
Pelekoudas, Chris, 86
Pena, Roberto, 133
Pepitone, Joe, 9, 12, 114
Perranoski, Ron, 8, 11, 13–14, 88, 95–96, 98, 113–115, 117, 119–121, 152
Philadelphia Phillies, 71, 136
Phillips, Bubba, 75
Phillips, Lefty, 118, 120
Piedmont League, 19
Pierce, Billy, 74, 80, 96
Pignatano, Joe, ix, 23, 67–68, 73
Pigtown, 1
Pinson, Vada, 84, 94
Pittsburgh Pirates, 8, 80
Podres, Anna, 15
Podres, Joan (Taylor), ix, 19–20, 108, 121
Podres, John Joseph, 15, 145
Podres, Joseph, 17–19, 57, 88
Podres, Joseph Michael, 122
Podres, Steven, 52
Polo Grounds, 3, 18, 63, 65, 68, 99
Port Henry, New York, 16, 57
Post, Wally, 94
Power, Myrt, 46

160

"pull the shade changeup," 22, 103, 107, 133
Purdin, John, ix, 116

R

Rabe, Charlie, 71
Reberger, Frank, 133
Reed, Howie, 116–117, 120–121
Reese, Pee Wee, 5, 15, 21, 23, 27–29, 41–42, 44–45, 49, 53, 64, 66, 71–72
Reiser, Pete, 91, 111
Republic Steel, 19, 57
Repulski, Rip, 71
Richert, Pete, ix, 115, 135
Rizzuto, Phil, 43, 52
Roberts, Robin, 18
Robinson, Frank, 63–64, 86, 94
Robinson, Jackie, 2, 5, 15, 21, 26, 41, 43, 53, 63, 69
Roe, Preacher, 3–5, 22, 24, 153
Roebuck, Ed, 18, 36, 97
Roosevelt Raceway, 27
Roseboro, John, 14, 69, 71–73, 76–77, 79, 88, 91, 94, 99, 112–114, 119, 123, 140
Rowe, Ken, ix, 93, 135
Rush, Bob, 73
Russell, Bill, 134
Ruth, Babe, 39–40

S

Saint Louis Cardinals, 39, 63, 71–72, 87, 95, 112–116, 133
Sanford, Jack, 96
Santa Anita Racetrack, 68, 83
San Diego Padres, xii, 104, 131, 133
San Francisco Giants, 8, 68, 70, 72, 94–98

Saratoga, New York, 27, 137
Sauer, Hank, 64
Savage, Ted, 95
Schilling, Curt, 27, 136–137
Scott, Lee, 83, 111
Scully, Vin, 4, 55, 73
Seals Stadium, 70
Seattle Pilots, 131
Seaver, Tom, 132
Selma, Dick, 131
Semproch, Ray, 81
Shaw, Bob ix, 74
Sheppard, Bob, 10, 43
Sherry, Larry, ix, 71–72, 74, 76–81, 84, 86–88, 92, 94, 96, 112–113, 122, 126–127, 153
Sherry, Norm, ix, 122
Shipstad & Johnston, 20
Short, Chris, 119
Shuba, George, 44–45, 48
Simmons, Curt, 18, 95
Sinatra, Frank, 68
Singer, Bill, 116, 125
Sisk, Tommie, 132
Sisler, Dick, 3
Sisler, George, 17
Skaff, Frank, 126
Skowron, Bill, 10, 14, 42–43, 48–49, 98, 115
Slaught, Don, 22
Smith, Al, 74–76, 78
Smith, Charlie, 119
Smith, Mayo, 127
Smith, Red, 45
Smith, Willie, 133
Smithson, Mike, 135
Snider, Duke, 4–5, 21, 28, 34, 42, 48–49, 53, 66, 69–71, 73, 76, 78, 80–81, 83, 87–88, 91, 96–97, 132

Snyder, Gene, 71
Spahn, Warren, 73, 85, 113
Sparma, Joe, 127–128
Spooner, Karl, 24, 42
Staley, Gerry, ix, 74
Stanley, Mickey, 127
Stengel, Casey, 24, 39
Stoneham, Horace, 68
Sutton, Don, xii, 6, 123, 152–153
Swift, Bob, 126
Swoboda, Ron, 134

T

Tampa Bay Devil Rays, 27, 92
Taylor, Ron, 115
Temple, Johnny, 64, 113
Terry, Ralph, 10
Texas Rangers, 135
Thompson, Fresco, 56
Thomson, Bobby, 3, 64
Torborg, Jeff, ix, 117, 133
Torgeson, Earl, 76
Torre, Frank, 73
Torre, Joe, 114
Torrez, Mike, 135
Tracewski, Dick, 10, 126
Tresh, Tom, 7, 10
Tudor, John, 135

V

Valdes, Rene, 65
Valley Field, Quebec, 17
Vance, Dazzy, 33, 94, 152
Veeck, Bill, 126
Vero Beach, 21–22, 62, 69–70, 80
Versalles, Zoilo, 121, 131
Viola, Frank, 135

W

Waddell, Rube, 113
Walker, Rube, 69
Walls, Lee, 91, 97–98
Wickersham, Dave, ix, 126
Willhite, Nick, 119
Williams, Joe, 46
Williams, Mitch, ix, 136–137
Williams, Stan, ix, 10, 69, 71, 74, 80, 84, 88, 92, 95–98
Williams, Ted, 61
Wills, Maury, 8–9, 14, 73, 75–76, 78, 81, 88, 91, 95–98, 112, 115, 117, 121, 123, 139–140
Wilson, Don, 132
Wilson, Earl, 126
Windhorn, Gordy, ix, 88
Witherbee, New York, 15, 34, 47, 145
Wolpin, Stewart, 55
Woods, Dr. Bob, 86
Wynn, Early, 74

Y

Young, Dick, 112

Z

Zeile, Todd, 22
Ziff, Sid, 111
Zimmer, Don, xi, 26–27, 43–45, 48, 53, 65, 68–69, 73–75, 91, 104, 134–135, 140

The Authors

Bob Bennett has attended Dodgers games in Ebbets Field, Dodger Stadium and Yankee Stadium. He watched Johnny Podres pitch his 1955 World Series victories and interviewed him later as a sports reporter. He was a newspaper reporter and magazine writer, editor and publisher and went on to become a book publishing marketing and sales executive as well as public relations and advertising manager for two Fortune 100 corporations in New York. He is the author of six non-fiction books produced by five different publishers. He holds a masters degree in American Studies from New York University.

John Bennett is a long-standing member of the Society for American Baseball Research and a contributor to its Baseball Biography Project. He is also a member of the Pro Football Researchers of America and the NFL Alumni Association. He is a contributing author of *Deadball Stars of the National League* (Brassey's Inc., 2004), *Green Mountain Boys of Summer* (New England Press, 2001), and the *2001 Big Bad Baseball Annual* (Red Herring Press, 2001). An active collector of sports memorabilia, he is a recognized expert in the field. He teaches history and social studies in Vermont. He earned a masters degree in Russian Area Studies from Georgetown University.

Robert S. Bennett is the author of *A Collector's Guide to Autographs* and *Collecting Original Cartoon Art* (Wallace Homestead, 1986, 1987), a contributing author of *Green Mountain Boys of Summer* (New England Press, 2001) and the author of more than 50 published articles on movies, sports, law and politics. His autograph collection was featured in *Business Week* in 1993. He is a lawyer with his own firm in New York, specializing in technology and intellectual property law. He holds a juris doctor degree from Albany Law School of Union University.